Towards an African Literature

THE EMERGENCE OF LITERARY FORM IN XHOSA

Perspectives on Southern Africa

Towards an African Literature

The Emergence of Literary Form in Xhosa

by

A. C. JORDAN

UNIVERSITY OF CALIFORNIA
PRESS

BERKELEY · LOS ANGELES · LONDON

1973

University of California Press
Berkeley and Los Angeles, California
University of California Press, Ltd.
London, England
Copyright © 1973, by
The Regents of the University of California
ISBN: 0-520-02079-0
Library of Congress Catalog Card Number: 75-165235
Printed in the United States of America

Contents

Introduction

AFRICAN literature today exists in a state of seeming paradox: more seems to have been written about it than actually exists. This outpouring of writings on African literature, and other things African, began in the late 1950s and early 1960s. By no mere coincidence, this is the period in which most of Africa became independent. While many of us are relieved by the fact that entrenched European colonialism has to a certain extent died out, a new menace has appeared on the scene: the American or European academician, with camera and tape recorder, running hither and thither, collecting material for his latest book on African literature. While the last statement might seem racist to some, let me add that the attempt to inform the world about the literature of Africa is to be applauded. However, most of the books on Africa by American and European academicians are far too superficial, because most of these scholars have only a superficial knowledge and understanding of Africa.

If literature reflects the society which produced it, then understanding the social forces at work in that society is vital to appreciating that society's literature. Unfortunately most of those who write about the literature of Africa are locked in ivory towers. Periodically they produce weighty dissertations on such subjects as how Achebe, Soyinka, La Guma, Rive, et al., place their commas, periods, colons, and quotation marks, and, for Southern Africa, ignore hundreds of writers who use the African languages, a medium quite foreign to most of the "experts." These scholars leave the study of the societies whose literature they are critizing to the anthropologist. One or two will, now and then, make a year-long foray into the "bush" and emerge with "new" material for another treatise. This colonialist and racist mentality—that it is easy for whites to understand "primitive" cultures, but impossible for a nonwhite to understand "advanced" cultures—is to a large extent responsible for the shoddy, exploitative writing on Africa today. What African literature needs is work by African scholars who know and understand the cultures and peoples of Africa.

Although it restricts itself to Southern African literature, *Towards an African Literature* is a step in that direction. The essays originally appeared in the 1950s in the now defunct quarterly, *Africa South,* which, though not strictly a literary magazine, carried some literary pieces. "The writer," says Maxim Gorky, "is like the eyes and ears of his epoch." By this I understand that a writer, being witness of his time, cannot yet be above it, as some critics would like us to believe. Like every member of society, the writer has a role to play. To be relevant, he must reflect the hopes and aspirations of his society, its struggles and tribulations, its triumphs and failures. But this, he can do, only if he is part and parcel of his society, which is the base on which he stands and from which he can draw sustenance. Unfortunately, in the colonial world, where two societies exist—the society of the colonizer and the society of the colonized—during the process of acculturation, many of the colonized become alienated from their indigenous society. But they soon find that the society of the colonizers is not prepared to accept them fully. Thus, the acculturated natives often find themselves in a no-man's-land with nowhere to go for inspiration.

The distinguishing characteristic of A. C. Jordan's *Towards an African Literature* is its approach to Southern African literature. The writers and their works are placed in their proper historical perspective. The events that helped shape present-day South Africa, the understanding of which is vital to understanding current South African literature, are recounted in detail. The effect these traumatic events had on African writers is dealt with at some length. This approach has led Jordan to choose certain writers to the total exclusion of others. He deals here with those writers who became the mouthpiece of the conquered African societies, men who sounded the clarion call to resistance—men like W. W. Gqoba, Jonas Ntsiko, "UHadi"—but he merely mentions Tiyo Soga, the prolific writer of the period under review and one of the best essayists in the Xhosa language, then and now. As I understand it, this is because Tiyo Soga's writings do not reflect the cries and anguish of the African people, but rather, are an exhortation to the people to join the new society, where Soga believed there was "abundance of life" for all. Soga did not live to see that there was no place for him and his people in the society of the colonizers. He died at the age of 42, at the beginning of the industrial revolution in South Africa, a revolution that was to unleash the fury of exploitation and oppression.

While there are those who do not agree with this dialectical approach to literature, it has its advantages. It requires the literary critic to have more than a nodding acquaintance with the peoples whose literatures he is criticizing. He has to know the historical forces that shaped that society. (In spite of any current fad in academia, literature does not exist in vacuo.) The dialectical approach also gives the reader a context in which to analyze both the literature and academic works on the literature.

Unfortunately, *Towards an African Literature* is not a complete work. The author died in 1968 while he was finishing it. Consequently, it ends with a chapter on the early 20th century. One can only hope that more scholars will consider seriously Jordan's approach to literary criticism.

Madison, Wisconsin   LINDI NELANI JORDAN
1971

1
The People and Their Languages

IN case the reader should be led to expect a survey of the literature of the entire continent of Africa, let it be explained at once that for purposes of this and subsequent articles under this heading, we focus our attention on literature as expressed through the media of the indigenous African languages spoken in the Union of South Africa and the neighbouring territories.

There are two major language groups in this area—Nguni and Sotho. The linguistic forms in each group are mutually intelligible. The Nguni group includes Xhosa, spoken mainly in the Cape Province, and Zulu, spoken mainly in Natal and Rhodesian Ndebels, as literary dialects. One of the non-literary dialects in this group is Swazi, spoken in Swaziland and the the Eastern Transvaal. In the Sotho group there are three literary dialects. These are Southern Sotho, mainly in Basutoland and in some parts of the Orange Free State, the Northern Cape and the Transvaal, Northern Sotho in the Transvaal, and Tswana mainly in Bechuanaland, in some parts of the Transvaal and the North-Western Cape. In the Union of South Africa and the High Commission Territories alone, there are approximately 5,000,000 Nguni-speaking and 3,000,000 Sotho-speaking people—approximately 8,000,000 in all. Besides these there are 133,000 Venda-speaking people in the Zoutpansberg district of the Transvaal and approximately 370,000 Tsonga-speaking, 350,000 of whom live in the Transvaal. There are therefore in this area 8,500,000 people whose mother tongue is a linguistic form belonging to one or another of these four language groups. These languages belong to that family of languages which, for purposes of linguistic classification, is known as the Bantu family. This family covers approximately the whole of the southern half of the continent of Africa, and consists of well over two hundred languages. While we deal mainly with the southern area, we wish to point out that many of the characteristics we are going to touch upon apply to the whole of the Bantu family.

African literature is, by modern world standards, only in its infancy. The purpose of the present essays is to give the reader an idea as to what promise there is of a grown-up literature. This we shall do by first of all showing what the African genius was able to achieve through the ages, independently of any outside influence. Then we shall go on to show what is being done, and possibly to suggest what could further be done under the influence of modern civilisation.

Traditional Literature

The history of the literature of the Southern Africans begins long before these people knew anything about writing and long before the advent of the European. Like other peoples of the world, the Africans gave artistic utterance to their deepest thoughts and feelings about those abstract and concrete things that came within their experience; to their speculation about the origin of things, including man himself and the universe; to their interpretation of the struggle between man and the mysterious forces that surrounded him, and to their admiration for those individuals of the human race to whom legend gave credit for the triumph of man over such forces; to their interest in the ways and habits of animals; to their traditional wisdom concerning conduct. Lastly, they gave "concrete and artistic expression . . . in emotional and rhythmical language" to their admiration for collective and individual courage and achievement in the mighty contests between clan and clan, between tribe and tribe.

Among other genres in these traditional possessions there are myths and legends, tales about ordinary folk, animal stories, proverbs, songs and lyrics and, lastly, praise-poems. In the present essay we can only deal with a few aspects of narrative prose, and we propose to leave out the myths and animal stories and deal with the tales about men and women; first, because in the experience of the writer, the English-speaking world knows far less about the latter, a great deal more attention having been paid to myths and animal stories by English translators, and secondly, because in the tales about people there is much greater variety of character and incident than in the other two.

Man Versus Monster

The world of African traditional literature is inhabited not only by man and animal, but also by ogres and other monsters—grotesque figures, so stupid that in spite of their superior physical powers, man triumphs over them. Some live on land and others in the deep black pools of large rivers. Those that live on land are usually half-man and half-beast. The best known of these is the *Zimu* (Nguni) or *Dimo* (Sotho). This is an ogre of enormous size. He swallows some animals alive, so that when he is asleep you can sometimes hear live lambs bleating and calves blaring in his vast stomach. At birth, this ogre has two legs, one sweet, the other bitter. His parents cut off the sweet leg and eat it up immediately after the birth of the baby-ogre. But on the remaining leg the grown-up ogre runs faster than the wind. The female Zimu is even more grotesque than the male. She has a tooth so long that "it reaches the other side of the river." She has breasts reaching as low as her knees. These ogres are man-eating, but their social system is in many ways similar to the social system of man. They have their own kings.

In one of the best known Zimu stories, a human

princess is chased and caught by a band of ogres. But they find her so beautiful that they decide not to kill and eat her, but carry her to their land and give her over to their king as wife. Although this young woman remains in the land of the ogres long enough to have a beautiful human daughter, she never accepts the disgusting ways of the ogres and never accepts her position as the wife of their king, and she sees to it that her daughter does not accept them either. Every day she sings of her brother, Mbhengu-sonyangashe, "Leader of Raiders, Prince of Embho and Nguniland, Who hits one buck with his mighty club, But fells the whole herd before his feet." So, the ogres are always on the lookout for Mbhengu-sonyangashe.

After many, many years, Mbhengu-sonyangashe reaches the land of the ogres all alone. He hides himself among the reeds on the bank of the river, very near the place where the girls come to draw water. A group of Zimu "girls" come to draw water. With them is the beautiful little human girl whom he recognizes immediately as his sister's daughter. While the young ogresses play about, this little girl breaks from them and plays "human games" by herself. So Mbhengu-Sonyangashe finds an opportunity to draw her attention. The little girl takes to him at once, because "you do not look like these ugly things, the Zimus. You look like Mama and myself." He cuts her beautiful reeds and carves them. These she must carry home with her. When she reaches her mother's hut with the water-pot on her head, she is to place the reeds across the doorway and insist that no one but her mother must come and help take the clay-pot off her head. Then, as her mother is sure to tramp on some of the reeds and break them while in the act of helping her, she must cry that her mother must go in person to cut her fresh reeds from the exact spot where these were found. The plan works out successfully and Mbhengu-sonyangashe comes face-to-face with his long-lost sister. They decide that he must go with her to the "Royal Place." He covers his whole body with mud and is so well disguised, so sorry-looking when he comes before the king of the ogres, that everybody believes it when the queen says that she brought him home as her *vavunge* (menial), in which case no one may do him harm.

One day, the ogres go hunting. Only an old crone is left behind. As soon as they are gone, Mbhengu-sonyangashe reveals himself as the great hunter, takes his sister and her daughter away, together with all the herds of cattle belonging to the ogres. The old ogress tries to raise the alarm, but her voice is too weak, and by the time the ogres realize what is happening, the Leader of Raiders has swum across a flooded river with his sister and niece on his back. And he has managed to get the cattle across too. When the ogres come, they implore him to help them cross. They assure him that they will not kill him. Pretending to be taken in by these assurances, the great hunter plaits a long thick rope, ties a big stone to one end, and swings that end to the other side of the river, while he holds the other end in his hands. The ogres immediately seize their end of the rope (as men do in a tug-of-war) and ask the hunter to tow them across. He tows them. But just when they are in the middle of the river, "the rope slips out of his hands" and all the ogres are swept away by the current and drowned.

In these tales you find not only heroes but heroines

too, many of them princesses. These are vigorous, re-sourceful, spirited girls of the Medea type.

A hunter prince named Tshalu-Tshalu wase Mgho (the Fleet-footed One of Embholand) is transformed into an eland by an enchantress, a princess whose love he has rejected. He loves another princess who is "as beautiful as the rising sun." When she gets to know this, she immediately takes command of her lover's followers. She leads them to a pool where all the herds of eland go to drink at a certain time of the day. There she collects bundles and bundles of firewood and makes a big fire. When the elands come, she commands the youths to call out aloud with one voice, "Tshalu-Tshalu wase Mbho!" As soon as they do so, the leader of the herd looks round sharply.

"Seize him and throw him into the fire at once!" the princess commands. The young men obey. When the eland has burnt out completely, the princess collects the ashes very carefully and mixes them with some enchanted ointment contained in an earthen bowl that she had brought with her. Tshalu-Tshalu wase Mbho comes to life again.

There are some tales about the Kings of the Waters, snake-like monsters that could make the rivers flow or dry at will. These monsters travel from one place to another in a cyclone. They are very much attracted to human girls and very often "call" them into the water by their powers and make them their wives.

On his return from a great hunt that lasted many moons, a prince named Tfulako is dying of thirst. He and his comrades come to a big river. Some of the hunters immediately stoop to drink. But as soon as Tfulako stoops, the river dries up completely. This goes on the whole day, while the hunters rest on the bank of the river and roast meat. At last, in sheer desperation, Tfulako calls out: "King of the Waters! I die of thirst. Allow me to drink, and I will give you my beautiful sister to be your wife." At once the river flows, and Tfulako drinks and quenches his thirst. When the hunters reach home, they report what has happened. Nobody has any idea what the King of the Waters looks like, but everybody, including the beautiful sister, feels that this is the only offer that Tfulako could have made in the circumstances. So they await the coming of the King of the Waters.

One afternoon, after some moons have died, a terrible cyclone approaches. It makes straight for the hut of the maidens where the princess and the other girls are, and it disappears and calm is restored. When the dust clears, the girls discover that they are in the company of a long, long snake, whose girth is greater than the thigh of a very big man. They realize that this must be the King of the Waters, come to claim his bride. One by one the girls leave the hut, until the princess is left alone with the bridegroom. When she turns to go, the King of the Waters quickly unfolds himself, coils himself round her body, rests his head on her breasts, and gazes longingly into her eyes.

The princess runs out of the hut with her burden round her body and, without consulting anybody, sets on a long, long journey to her mother's people. As she goes she sings in a high, thin voice:

Shall I, the child of the people of Tfulako,
Shall I, the child of the people of Tfulako,
Sleep with that which is called a snake, a snake?

voice:

Long and graceful though I am, so long, so graceful,
Long and graceful though I am, so long and so
   graceful,
May I not sleep with that which is called a woman,
   a woman?

And so they travel through forest and ravine, the whole
night and the following day, singing pride at each
other.

At nightfall they reach the home of her mother's
people. But the princess waits in the shadows until she
is sure that there is no one in the hut of the maidens.
Then she enters there unnoticed. She asks the King of
the Waters to undo himself and rest while she goes to
make herself beautiful. She goes to the great hut and
explains everything to her mother's brother and his
wife, and then asks them to give her some ointment.
She anoints her body very freely, and then covers herself with a beautiful kaross and returns to the hut of the
maidens alone. Once inside, she throws off the kaross
and invites the King of the Waters to embrace her. He
accepts eagerly, but the princess's body is so slippery
that for all his scales he cannot hold her. She then offers
to go and remove the ointment. Again he accepts eagerly. The princess picks up her kaross, walks out of the
hut, closes and fastens the door very securely from
outside. Then she sets the hut on fire, and the King of
the Waters is burnt to death.

Man and Animal

In these stories there is seldom, if ever, any conflict
between man and the ordinary animals. (The hunting

of animals by man, which is very often incidental to the encounters with the monsters, would seem to belong to a different "universe.") Far from being hostile to man, the animal, especially the small ones, often come to his help in the contests with monsters.

A group of young men, on approaching the house of a dangerous sorcerer named Ngangezulu (As-great-as-the-heavens), meet a mouse who persuades them to flay him and take his "talking skin" with them, so that it may give the alarm when danger is near.

Birds, especially doves in pairs, figure a good deal in stories about ordinary folk and babies. In one story, the doves find a young married woman weeping because she cannot beget children. The doves advise her to make two little loaves of bread, equal in size, and leave them uncovered in a clay-pot for five days. She carries out their advice, and when she looks into the pot after five days, she finds not loaves of bread, but beautiful twin babies.

Then there is the story of the beautiful Sikhamba-nge-nyanga (She-who-walks-by-moonlight). This was a girl, so beautiful that if she stepped into the light of day, the men would not go hunting, the women would not go to hoe the lands, the girls would not go and draw water from the river, and the herd-boys would not drive the cattle to the pastures, and the animals, too, would not go to the pastures. All living things would flock where she was and gaze at her, feasting their eyes on her beauty. She was therefore not to come out during the day. She came out by moonlight and went to draw water from the river by moonlight, when all people had finished their day's work and could gaze at her.

When She-who-walks-by-moonlight got married, her people-in-law were warned to observe this custom. They did so and all went well until the baby was born. Then one day, all the people of the house went out to work in the fields, leaving the young mother with her baby and the *mpelesi* (nurse girl sent especially by her mother's people). Besides them there was an old, old woman who was too weak to help herself in any way. In the middle of the day, the old woman felt very thirsty. Sikhamba-nge-nyanga gave her some water, but it was not fresh, and the old woman would not drink it. So Sikhamba-nge-nyanga was forced to pick up the water pot and the ladle, step into the light of day and go to draw water from the river.

She tried to draw water with the ladle, but it slipped out of her hand and disappeared. She tried to draw with the water-pot itself, but it slipped out of her hand and disappeared. She took off her headcover to immerse in the water and carry home quickly so that the thirsty woman could suck the water from it. But this, too, slipped out of her hands and disappeared. She cupped her hands and tried to draw some water with them. Then she disappeared under the water. Her people-in-law did all they could to recover her, in vain. Meanwhile the baby was hungry and crying for its mother.

At moonrise the mpelesi, without telling any of the in-laws, carried the baby to the edge of the pool where the mother had disappeared and sang a sad song, calling on the mother to come out and suckle the baby. Sikhamba-nge-nyanga came out, suckled and fondled her baby and without saying a word, handed it back to the mpelesi and disappeared. This went on for a number of

days until the in-laws discovered it. Then the men
decided to go and waylay the mother. They hid themselves among the reeds near the pool and heard the
mpelesi sing her sad song, saw the mother come out of
the water, saw her suckle her baby. And just as she was
handing it back, they sprang upon her, seized her and
would carry her home. But the river followed them,
followed them beyond the reeds, followed them
through the woods, beyond the woods, up the slope,
right up to the village. Then the people were seized
with fear and they put her down, and the river received
her and receded to its place.

When the people were at a loss what to do, two
doves appeared and offered to fly to Sikhamba-nge-
nyanga's own people, report what had happened and
seek advice. On reaching her home the doves perched
on the gate-posts of the cattlefold. When the herdboys
saw them, they wanted to kill them in order to roast
them and eat them. But the doves sang:

> We are not doves that may be killed
> We come to tell of her that walks by moonlight;
> She dipped the ladle, and it went down,
> She dipped the pot, and it went down,
> She dipped her headcover, and it went down,
> She dipped her hands, and then she went down.

The people gave the doves some corn to eat, and then
asked them to fly back swiftly and tell Sikhamba-nge-
nyanga's in-laws to slaughter and flay a dun-coloured
ox and throw its carcass into the pool after nightfall.
The doves flew back quickly and delivered their message. The order was carried out.

At moonrise that night, when the mpelesi carried the

baby to the water's edge, all the people of the village followed her. They heard her sing her sad song, and they saw Sikhamba-nge-nyanga come out of the water and suckle and fondle her baby. But this time, after the baby had been fed, the mother did not hand it back to the mpelesi. Instead she carried it lovingly in her arms. And she walked quietly back to the village, the people gazed and gazed and gazed at her beauty in the moon-light.

It will have been noted that most of the factors that constitute the subject matter of the great human litera-ture are to be found in rudimentary form in these tales: courage and resourcefulness; love and readiness to sac-rifice for one's loved ones; the vindictiveness of de-spised love; the power and influence of beauty; conflict of duties (Sikhamba-nge-nyanga's duty to the commu-nity conflicting with her duty to the old woman who is dying of thirst); retribution for upsetting the moral or social order; the triumph of brain over brawn; the triumph of good over evil. If these and many other tales of this kind have survived through the ages, it is be-cause of their artistic value, each one of them symboliz-ing something of permanent meaning to man as man. Evidence of this permanance is to be found not only in the hyperbolic language of the traditional praise-poems, in which mighty men are very often likened to fabulous monsters, but also in the living language of every day, in the numerous idiomatic expressions, proverbs, and aphorisms, many of which are based on the characters and incidents of the traditional tale.

The few specimens that have been given here will have shown that African soil is by no means barren. When overseas critics complain that South African art, in any form, lacks local character, is it not probably because the cultural world is looking for just these and other traditional artistic possessions, of which South Africa itself has not become aware? Would not some of these tales and songs provide great themes for symphonic poems, opera, ballet? Would not a South African poet or painter, whether Black or White, find as inspiring a theme in She-who-walks-by-moonlight as English poets and painters found in the Lady of Shalott? One can only hope that by the time South Africa develops a correct attitude to human culture, at least some of these treasures will still be there for genius to utilize and leave as a legacy to humanity.

2
Traditional Poetry

IN the Introduction to his *Zulu-Kafir Diction-ary* (1857), the Rev. J. L. Döhne, Missionary to the American Board, writes as follows:

Some have expected to find much poetry among the Zulu-Kafirs, but there is, in fact, none. Poetical language is extremely rare, and we meet with only a few pieces of prose. The Zulu nation is more fond of "ukuhlabela," i.e., singing, and engage more in "ukuvuma amagama ezinkosi," i.e., singing the praises of the chiefs, than any other Kafir tribe. But their capabilities in this respect are very limited. The highest song of praise for their king is composed of a few hyperbolical expressions. Other specimens consist of the frequent repetition of one sentence ... regarding some object, such as a cow, a dog, a dance, a girl, repeated in a singing voice—or they are a mere imitation of a roaring war noise, that of a wild savage animal, of the clashing of shields or spears. But nothing like poetry or song exists—no metre, no rhyme, nothing that interests or soothes the feelings or arrests the passions —no admiration of the heavenly bodies, or taste for the beauties of creation. We miss the cultivated mind which delights in seizing on these subjects and embodying them in suitable language.

According to his own account of himself, Döhne worked for ten years amongst the Xhosa-speaking people in the Eastern Cape before going to Zululand. His dictionary was published after ten years of work amongst the Zulu-speaking, that is, after twenty years of work amongst several peoples who spoke one or other of the mutually intelligible Nguni dialects. There can be no doubt that during that period Döhne acquired a working knowledge of Nguni in general, and of Zulu in particular. His flat denial of the existence of poetry amongst the Zulu-speaking people can therefore be attributed not to a lack of understanding of the language, but to his conception of poetry. This conception is implied, rather than stated. Apparently, on looking for trochoes, dactylic hexameters, iambic pentameters, rhyme schemes, etc., and not finding them, Döhne should have forgiven the Zulu bards if at least they had composed some poems dealing directly with the stars, the moon, and the Milky Way. Having looked for these in vain, he concludes that there is no poetry. In Döhne's pronouncement one is reminded of that attitude, so well described by Otto Jespersen, of "men fresh from grammar-school training" towards language. To these men,

no language would seem really respectable that had not four or five distinct cases and three genders, or that had less than five tenses and as many moods in its verbs. Accordingly, such poor languages as had either lost much of their original richness in grammatical forms . . . or had never had any . . . so far as one knew . . . were naturally looked upon with something of the pity bestowed on relatives in reduced circumstances, or the contempt felt for foreign paupers.

Watts-Dunston defines poetry as "the concrete and artistic expression of the human mind in emotional and rhythmical language." Accepting this definition, as we do, for our present purpose, we find that in the indigenous languages of Southern Africa, including Zulu, there is a wealth of traditional poetry covering, in its subject matter, the whole range of human experience and emotion—of the young child excited about the "funny" movements of the frog, or curious about the timid little bird that hops and flutters about from twig to twig; of the youth in the joys and pangs of love; of the vigorous hunter or warrior; of the aging man longing to rest with his fathers in the land of the spirits; of the clan or tribe reliving its past tribulations and triumphs, etc.

These emotional experiences are expressed communally in song, speech, and action. There is therefore a strong dramatic element, and to draw a dividing line between the lyrical and the dramatic is impossible. We can, however, make two divisions, namely, *lyric and dramatic verse,* which includes nursery rhymes and jingles and all the various kinds of songs, e.g., love-songs, work-songs, hunting-songs, war-songs, etc., and *praise-poems.* The latter is a genre for which no exact parallel is to be found either in classical or in modern Western poetry. In spirit, content and form, it partakes of the features of the epic on the one hand, and of those of the ode on the other. In general, Bantu traditional poetry has much in common with Hebrew poetry. There is no "regular metre" in the classical sense, but there is

marked rhythm achieved, inter alia, by means of bal-
ance of thought.

Lyric and Dramatic Verse

In some songs, the words are more important than the
tune, while in others there is little or no meaning in the
"words." Generally in a song there is a leader and a
chorus. If the words are very important, they fit into
the part sung by the leader, and the chorus takes up a
refrain, either in some meaningful word or words related to the main theme, or in meaningless, monosyl-
labic ejaculations like *fa la la* or *ho ho ho*.

In the following love-song, the Xhosa girl yearns for
an absent lover:

> The far-off mountains hide you from me,
> While the nearer ones overhang me;
> Would that I had a heavy sledge
> To crush the mountains near me;
> Would that I had wings like a bird
> To fly over those farther away.

The Xhosa young man who looks forward to meeting
the girl he loves after a strenuous day's work apost-
rophizes her as follows:

> Shade wherein I rest when I am weary,
> Fount whereof I drink when I am thirsty.

The prospect of a mother-in-law is seldom a pleasant
one. The Hlubi girl who would rather continue to enjoy
her youthful freedom than get married, sings appealingly:

Alas!
No more daydreams, tall proud maiden!
O father! O mother!
Why marry me off so young?
Think of her who is not my mother,
How is she likely to handle me?

But there is the other Hlubi girl, to whom even the
prospect of a cruel mother-in-law pales into insignifi-
cance as she realizes how fast she herself is aging;

Come, it is late in the day!
All those of my age are married,
And now I wander, wander all alone.
Hold back the sun that it may not go down
Without carrying the news (of my betrothal to some
one).

The song of the aging maid is highly dramatic. As
they sing, the leader and the chorus hold their hands
appealingly to one side, and they sway their hips from
side to side with graceful modesty. Meanwhile the
young men, who hum the bass softly in sympathy,
walk slowly in a row along the line of girls and gaze
tenderly into the face of each one, especially that of the
leader.

But the very next day, these young men might be
miles away from these scenes of love, out in the wilds
after big game, and some of them might never return.
As they left the royal place, they used to announce
their departure on such an expedition with a hunting-
song. One of these is a famous buffalo-hunt song, ver-
sions of which are to be found amongst the Hlubi and
the Zulu:

Ye ha he! Ye ha he!
A mighty whirlwind, the buffalo!
Make for your homes, you who fear him.
They chase them far! They chase them near!
As for us, we smite the lively ones
And we leave the wounded alone.
Ye ha he! Ye ha he!
A mighty whirlwind, the buffalo!
The Zulu warriors used to salute their king as
 follows:
  Bayede!
Thou art the heavens,
  Thou, elephant-born!

But the kings had ideas of a heaven elsewhere—life of peace and quiet in the land of the spirits of their royal ancestors. So to these ancestors they used to offer the following prayer:

Hear thou, O King, tallest among the tall!
Offspring of Mandondo Gumede, most beautiful!
I linger here to beg of thee, first-born:
Let us weave us a rope, O'Mandi, son of Jama,
And go to heaven where the evil may not climb,
For should they try, they break their tiny toes.

The idiom, style, and technique of the traditional lyric are easily adaptable to new conceptions. We have evidence of this in a Xhosa hymn composed by Ntsikana, the first convert to Christianity. Ntsikana was completely illiterate. Before he was converted, he was a diviner and a great leader of dance and song. The hymn that he composed was accompanied by dancing and singing in the traditional manner:

Thou great God that dwellest in Heaven,
Thou art the shield, the stronghold of truth;

'Tis Thou, and Thou alone, that dwellest in the
  highest,
Thou the maker of life and the skies,
Thou the maker of the sparse and clustered stars,
As the shooting-star doth proclaim.
The horn soundeth aloud, calling us
To Thee, great Hunter, Hunter of souls,
Who maketh one herd of friend and foe,
All covered and sheltered under Thy cloak.
Thou art the little Lamb, Mesiyas,
Whose hands are wounded with nailing,
Whose feet are wounded with nailing,
Thy blood that streameth for ever and ever
For the sake of us men was shed.

Praise-Poems

To the Bantu-speaking Southern Africans, the praise-
poem is their proudest artistic possession. It is in this
genre that the greatest possibilities of a Bantu language
as a medium of literary expression are to be found.

The subject of a praise-poem may be a nation, a tribe,
a clan, a person, an animal, or a lifeless object. The
poem may be partly narrative, or partly or wholly de-
scriptive. It abounds in epithets, very much like the
Homeric ones, and the language in general is highly
figurative.

The bard, who was both composer and public reciter,
was versed in tribal history and lore, as well as being
witty. He held a position of honour in his community.
It was therefore the greatest ambition of every boy to
be at least a public reciter, if not a composer. In fact,
every boy was expected at the very least to be able to
recite his own praises, those of the family bull, those
of the favourite family cow, even if composed by

someone else, and was also expected to know the traditional praises of certain species of animals and birds. Any boy who lacked these accomplishments was held in contempt by the men as well as by other boys.

Rubusana's anthology of Xhosa praise-poems includes the "praises" of a boy who knew *Rhini* (Grahamstown), *Qonce* (King William's Town) and *Tinarha* (Uitenhage). On finding at these work centres that all the men had to be at work in the morning at six o'clock, the boy composed a poem in "praise" of himself:

> A mighty bell is six o'clock!
> I went to Rhini and found the men
> Driven by six o'clock;
> I went to Qonce and found the men
> Toiling at six o'clock;
> Back at Tinarha I found the men
> Bullied by six o'clock.

The boy is obviously having a dig at the men. He is amazed and amused to discover that there are places in the world where these supposed "gods" are so helpless and powerless as to be enslaved by a mysterious sound named "six o'clock!" His literary effort may seem puerile, but in essence the conception here is not different from that of the "machines of the mines" that enslave "the tribes of the Black One" in Vilkazi's poem. But there is something more. In suggesting that he himself is "six o'clock," the boy is cleverly insinuating that he is mightier than any man in the community.

In the experience of the present writer, the tradition of the praise-poem is strongest amongst the Hlubi. Now scattered all over Southern Africa, the Hlubi were once upon a time the most powerful of the Nguni tribes.

Their power was broken after the death of the legendary Bhungane. Of the sons of Bhungane the most famous was Mpangazitha (Despoiler-of-the-enemy), who held his own section of the Hlubi together for a long time in the era of Shaka. His downfall was brought about by internal quarrels. Betrayed by one of his half-brothers, he was defeated and killed by the Ngwane chief, Matiwane, on the banks of the Caledon.

Every clan among the Hlubi has its own praises. These make reference to heroic incidents in the history of the particular clan. The language is very hyperbolic, and "the sea" often means nothing more than a big river. From their praises, it is clear that the Hlubi tribe consisted of once independent clans who came together under various circumstances, thus swelling the numbers of some magnificent chief.

In order to join the Hlubi, the Masingila clan had to fight their way across one of the big rivers that flow into the Indian Ocean. They slew so many of the enemy that the water turned red. They are therefore praised as follows:

Beautiful as the blades of grass in summer
They came, from the seas, the blood-red sea,
That mighty river unfordable to men,
Crossed only by swallows, because they have wings.

The Rhadebe clan, whose brave sons are always ready to lay down their lives in defence of their homes:

They whose gates are not barred with poles,
But barred with the heads of warrior-men.
The Nozulu clan, whose daughters are famous for
    their beauty:

The beautiful Nguni of the Mother-of-the-heavens,
Who came fresh and beautiful as the cornfields in
    autumn.
Smooth and bright as the round stones of the river.

In this last one, the Hlubi pay compliments to the mother of the famous Mpangazitha. She belonged to this clan. The legend is that her people came as refugees to the Hlubi. In order to enter Hlubi territory, they had to cross a big river. To make sure that they should be welcome, the parents decided to dress all the beautiful girls as attractively as possible and let them go ahead of the rest of the group. The girls crossed the river and took a path through the cornfields. It was autumn. When the Hlubi saw these young women emerge from the fields, their admiration knew no bounds. "As beautiful as the cornfields themselves!" exclaimed one. "As smooth as the stones of the river they have just crossed!" observed another.

When the rest of the fugitives saw how kindly the girls were received, they decided to follow. On reaching the royal place, they were told, "If you are related to such beautiful young women, you cannot be bad people. We welcome you!" Mpangazitha's mother was a descendant of the leader of this fugitive clan.

So much for the praises of clans. We now proceed to give extracts from the praises of the chiefs.

The praises of Mpangazitha, leader of the Hlubi:
The Despoiler-of-the-enemy, kinsman of Jobe,
He is the clearing-and-frowning skies,
A thunderer like the heavens above,
Ever smiting man, but never decried;
He is the thudding myriads of Zikode and Dloma
That came thudding amidst the land.

Till all the nations quaked with fear;
He is the wielder of the brain-weighted club,
The true guardian of his people.
He is the fleetfooted buck of Mashiya and Dlomo
That gores as it dashes along.

Shaka, King of the Zulus:

He is Shaka the unshakable,
Thunderer-while-sitting, son of Menzi;
He is the bird that preys on other birds,
The battle-axe that excels other battle-axes;
He is the long-strided-pursuer, son of Ndaba,
Who pursued the moon and the sun;
He is a great hubbub like the rocks of Nkandla
Where the elephants take shelter
When the heavens frown.
'Tis he whose spears resound causing wailings,
Thus old women shall stay in abandoned homes,
And old men shall drop by the wayside.

Apart from describing the hero in general terms, a praise poem may devote some lines to narrating specific exploits in the life of the subject of praise. Lerotholi, grandson of Moshoeshoe ("moshesh") and hero of the Gun War (1880–1881), has his triumph recorded as follows:

Deep in his pool the crocodile glared,
He glared with his blood-red eyes,
And lo! the young White braves were drowned,
Aye, they fell into the jaws of the snake,
The black snake, khanyapa, King of the Waters

Khanyapa, King of the Waters, is supposed to have the power to "call" people into the deep pool where he lives, by merely glaring at them. But these powers are sometimes attributed also to the crocodile, *Koena,* which is the totem of the House of Moshoeshoe.

Ncaphayi, leader of the Bhaca, was famous for his skill in jungle warfare. His favourite tactic was to make his men retreat into a forest or jungle in a seemingly disorderly manner, as if routed. But in a short time, the pursuing enemy would find themselves encircled by the Bhaca. Ncaphayi used this tactic against the Mpondomise and defeated them, slaying their leader, Velelo, below the Nqadu mountain-forest (about fifteen miles east of the Umtata River). So,

> He is the light feather arching and vanishing
> Only to feast on men below the Nqadu mountain;
> He is the jungle-home of leopards and lions.

But it must not be thought that these bards were mere flatterers. While they drew attention mainly to the good and praiseworthy, they also had the license to make sharp criticisms of the habits of their subjects. It is here that the bard has found the greatest scope for his wit.

Dingane, murderer and successor of Shaka, was mean and greedy, always having a ready excuse to "eat up" the cattle of his wealthy subjects:

> He is the needy offspring of Mpikazi,
> With eye forever case on the people's herds;
> His cattle are gathered like honey-combs,
> Found and seized wherever he goes.

Luhadi, chief of the Bomvana, was very licentious:

> Below the rocks it is dreadful to behold,
> For there are the handsome and their concubines.

Ngangelizwe, chief of the Thembu, was so tyrannical that many of his subjects fled to other lands:

> See how the doves flutter and huddle,
> Dismayed at the sight of the eagle.
> Woe to the dove that has no wings!

There are some modern Bantu-speaking poets who seem to think that the praise-poem has had its day. But there are others who have shown very successfully that the idiom, style and technique of the traditional praise-poem can be applied most effectively to modern themes. Among the latter is the Xhosa poet, Mqhayi. When the Prince of Wales visited South Africa in 1925, Mqhayi "praised" him, and in the "praises" he apostrophized Britain as follows:

> Ah, Britain! Great Britain!
> Great Britain of the endless sunshine!
> She hath conquered the oceans and laid them low;
> She hath drained the little rivers and lapped them
>   dry;
> She hath swept the little nations and wiped them
>   away;
> And now she is making for the open skies.
> She sent us the preacher; she sent us the bottle,
> She sent us the Bible, and barrels of brandy;
> She sent us the breechloader, she sent us cannon;
> O, Roaring Britain! Which must we embrace?
> You sent us the truth, denied us the truth;
> You sent us the life, deprived us of life;
> You sent us the light, we sit in the dark,
> Shivering, benighted in the bright noonday sun.

3
Riddles and Proverbs

IN African traditional literature, the riddle and the proverb have much in common. Both are based upon common experience and both are presented in symbolic form. The riddle presents a mental problem. The proverb is a criticism of life. Both are products of the popular mind and therefore both reflect prevalent attitudes. But while the riddle is hardly more than a form of entertainment, the proverb is more serious and has a didactic intent. Hence riddling is associated mainly with the younger people, while the propounding and expounding of proverbs is associated with the older people, especially the men.

Riddles

1. The Enigma
The most popular type of African riddle (called *igh-ina,* 'a knot' in Xhosa) is like the enigma of Classical

Greece. The 'knot' is concealed under obscure language, and whoever has to 'untie' it must grasp the
associations or similarities. The subject may be anything within common experience—man, parts of the
human body, animals, plant life, the heavenly bodies,
etc.

In the following specimens the solution is indicated
in the brackets:

(1) "I have twin sons standing on either side the edge
of a mountain-forest in case it tumbles down."
[human ears, head and hair]

(2) "I have an old crone standing all alone in the
centre of a vast plain." [the human navel]

(3) "I have a woman who carries a bearded baby on
her back." [maize-stalk, maize-cob covered with
female filaments]

(4) "I have a sack full of corn. The corn is thrown
away and the sack is cooked and eaten." [the
stomach of a ruminating animal cooked as tripe]

(5) "I have a woman. She has many children and
they are to be seen covering a great plain with the
mother in their midst. But whenever her husband approaches, she and her children hide
away." [the moon, the stars and the sun]

Since the solution must always be given, some of the
riddles become so hackneyed that very often the solution is screamed out even before the proposing is complete. But every fresh experience in life provides scope
for originality, and every new riddle is greeted with
delight and admiration. Modern civilization has therefore enriched this field: "I have four people, two walk-
ing abreast ahead, and the other two following abreast
and trying to catch up with those ahead. But whenever

the front pair decides to wait, those following behind stop dead where they are" [the wheels of an ox-waggon or motor-car].

It is interesting to find that the famous riddle proposed by the Greek Sphinx to Oedipus is known to many Africans. What is more, many who have never heard it before are able to solve it as soon as it has been presented. It has slight variations: "I have an animal. In the morning (or at sunrise) it goes on four feet; at noon it goes on two; in the afternoon (at sunset or at nightfall) it goes on three".

2. The Bird Riddle

The essence of the bird riddle is to display one's knowledge of the ways and habits and/or colour-markings of the birds. It takes the form of a dialogue between two young men, or boys, in the presence of an audience. Instead of 'tying a knot', the proposer makes an assertion about a certain bird, likening it to a certain type of person. His interlocutor, who plays the part of a challenger, calls upon the proposer to point out the associations or similarities. This form of entertainment gives plenty of scope for wit and humour.

In the following specimens Ch.=Challenger, Pro.=-Proposer:

CH.: Do you know the birds?
PRO.: I do know the birds.
CH.: What bird do you know?
PRO.: I know the wagtail.
CH.: What about him?
PRO.: That he is a shepherd.
CH.: Why so?

PRO.: Because he is often to be seen amongst the flock.

The Challenger must all the time pretend not to be impressed. So, as soon as the likeness has been established, he says deprecatingly, "Ugh, you don't know the birds!" The Proposer replies emphatically, "I say I do know the birds!" Then they start again on some other bird:

"I know the owl . . . That he is a sorcerer . . . Because he always comes out in the depths of night to kill other animals."

"I know the butcher-bird . . . That he is a hunter and smeller-out of sorcerers . . . Because he impales the weaker birds and insects on thorn-bushes."

"I know the female dove . . . That she is a lazy woman . . . Because instead of building a nest she collects a few twigs and lays her eggs on them."

"Again I know the female dove . . . That she is a jealous wife . . . Because she never allows her husband to go out without her."

When the Proposer has 'spent all his philosophys', he accuses his interlocutor of not knowing the birds, and thus becomes the Challenger. The interlocutor immediately accepts the challenge and says that he does know the birds. Then they go on. At the end the audience have to say who is the winner. But here freshness of idea, wit and humour count more than just the number of birds named. Some associations and similarities are so commonplace that even a child could discover them, i.e., the wagtail and the shepherd. A competitor who brought out the following was declared the winner even though he had no other birds to name on that day:

CH.: What bird do you know?

Pro.: I know the white-necked raven.

Ch.: What about him?

Pro.: That he is a missionary.

Ch.: Why so?

Pro.: Because he wears a white collar and a black cassock, *and is always looking for dead bodies to bury!*

Proverbs

In general African proverbs state universally accepted principles and give guidance as to conduct in particular circumstances. Some proverbs are self-explanatory, but most are couched in symbolic terms. The latter draw largely from animal life, many of them being related to well-known fables (animal stories). Indeed, while many proverbs are derived from fables, there are a few fables that would seem to have been created to illustrate existing proverbs.

The following specimens are drawn from the Nguni (Xhosa-Zulu), the Tsonga (Ronga-Tswa, etc.), and the Sotho (Sotho-Tswana) groups of languages. The language-group is indicated only in those cases where the writer is not sure if the particular proverb is to be found in the other two. Those that are not marked are to be found in all three groups, word for word. Where the fundamental idea is the same but expressed in different ways, this is indicated too.

Self-explanatory

(1) "A chief is no chief to his own wife".

(2) "Where there is no wealth there is no poverty" (Sotho).

(3) "Wealth and poverty lie together" (Nguni and Sotho).

Symbolic

(1) "A baby that does not cry dies in the skin-shawl (on its mother's back)". I.e., if you would have your grievances redressed, voice them without fear.

(2) "The cow kicks the one who milks it" (Nguni). "The buffalo goes for the one who hunts it" (Tsonga). "The fire burns those who sit by it" (Sotho). I.e., trouble comes to those who court it.

(3) "The elephant does not die of one broken rib" (Tsonga). I.e., a strong man is not crushed by one piece of misfortune.

(4) "The sweat of the dog dries in his own hair (or skin)". I.e., the efforts of an obscure person are never acknowledged, however heroic they may be.

The following are related to fables:

"The Rock-rabbit has no tail because he trusted to others (to bring him one)". After the creation, when all the animals were invited to come and receive their tails, the Rock-rabbit, preferring to sit and bask in the sun, requested the Monkey to bring him a tail. But on being supplied with the extra tail, the Monkey decided to add it on to his own. Hence, the "knot" on the Monkey's tail. This proverb exhorts people to do things themselves and not to trust to others to do things for them.

The Hare, pursued relentlessly by the Lion, took refuge in a small hole. Unable to enter, the Lion stood over the hole. But he soon noticed that the sight of his whiskers was enough to set the Hare trembling. So he pulled off his whiskers, placed them over the hole and went away. Every time the Hare tried to venture out, he saw the whiskers and quickly withdrew into the hole where he eventually died of hunger. "Do not be scared by the Lion's whiskers" (i.e., do not panic over a false alarm).

4
The Dawn
of Literature
Among the Xhosa

IN all the speech communities of the Southern Africans, what literacy exists is inseparably bound up with Christian missionary enterprise. To be able to "preach the Word" the missionaries had not only to learn the languages of the people, but also reduce these languages to writing. Translators, interpreters, preachers, and teachers had sooner or later to come from among the aborigines themselves. And so some of the apt converts had also to be introduced to the rudiments of modern learning through the medium of the language of the missionary body concerned. But since, outside of the missionary bodies, no one undertook to educate the Africans, acceptance of "the Word" remained the only means of access to any form of modern learning, and literacy became the exclusive privilege of a few Christian converts and their progeny.

The dawn of literacy is to be associated, first and foremost, with the Glasgow Missionary Society, whose representatives reduced the Xhosa language to writing at a small mission station on the banks of the Tyhume (Eastern Province) in 1821. The first man ever to write a book in Xhosa was John Bennie, one of the three Glasgow missionaries who founded Lovedale.

Some time before the coming of the Glasgow Mission, Ntsikana[1] had caught the spirit of the Christian religion from the preachings of Dr. van der Kemp and, indeed, had founded his own Church. Ntsikana refused to be baptized by the Glasgow Missionaries, but on his deathbed expressed the wish that his followers should take their families and his two wives and sons to the mission station at Gwali (Old Lovedale). It is to these converts that we owe the life story of Ntsikana, and it is to their sons that we are indebted for the earliest record of anything ever written by a Xhosa-speaker in Xhosa. So it is that the earliest record of anything ever written by any Bantu-speaking African in his own language in Southern Africa was made at the small printing press at Old Lovedale about the end of the first quarter of the 19th century.

The earliest writings appeared in a periodical called *Ikwezi* (The Morning Star), published by the mission, and were done by those first converts who must have learned to read and write in their old age. By 1862, when *Indaba* (The News) succeeded *Ikwezi,* the first truly literate generation of Xhosa speakers was in a position to make contributions whose literary merit established once and for all the status of this dialect as the literary medium, not only of the original Xhosa-speaking people, but also of the Mbho people (so-called "Fingos") who found sanctuary with the Xhosa

1. See *Africa South,* Vol. 2, No. 1, pp. 100–101.

about 1834, and of other sections of the Nguni whom literacy was beginning to reach through various missionary bodies throughout the Cape Province.

The leading figure amongst the contributors to *Indaba* was Tiyo Soga, a brilliant son of Ntsikana's most trusted friend and convert. Tiyo Soga was sent to Scotland in 1846 with the sons of the the missionaries Ross and Thomson for further education, and he returned to South Africa an ordained minister of religion in 1857. His famous hymn, *Lizalis' Idinga Lakho* (Fulfil Thy Promise) was composed when the author landed on African soil on his return from Scotland. But his greatest contribution to Xhosa literature was *Uhambo lo Mhambi,* an excellent translation of the first part of *The Pilgrim's Progress,* which has had almost as great an influence on the Xhosa language as the Authorized Version of the Bible upon English. In 1868, he was elected to a Revision Board whose task it was to prepare a revised version of the Xhosa Bible, and was engaged in translating *The Acts of the Apostles* when he died in 1871, at the early age of forty-two.

Among Tiyo Soga's younger contemporaries was a versatile man named William W. Gqoba. Originally a waggon-maker by trade, Gqoba became editor of *Isigidimi Sama-Xhosa* (The Xhosa Messenger), a periodical that succeeded Indaba in 1870. Gqoba collected a large number of Xhosa proverbial and idiomatic expressions, and excellent prose. He also wrote some history, confining himself to specific episodes like the scattering of the tribes in the Shaka era and the Nongqawuse cattle-killing episode of 1856–1857; and some verse, including two didactic poems, one on Paganism versus Christianity, 850 lines, and the other on Education, 1,150 lines. Gqoba died in 1888 at the age of forty-eight. Some of his writings appeared in *Isigidimi* during his lifetime. The rest appeared eighteen years after his death in an anthology of prose and poetry, *Zemk' Inkomo Magnalandini!* (Preserve your heritage!), collected and edited by W. B. Rubusana and published in 1906.

Two periodicals appeared almost simultaneously in 1897. These were *Imvo Zabantsundu* (The Opinions of the Blacks), edited by John Tengo Jabavu, and *Izwi Labantu* (The Voice of the People), edited by Nathaniel Cyril Mhala. Rubusana was closely associated with *Izwe Labantu,* and much of the material in his anthology originally appeared in this periodical.

A much younger writer who began to draw attention when *Imvo* and *Izwe* flourished was S. E. Krune Mqhayi,[2] a man destined to carry the literary tradition into its second phase. Journalist, poet, novelist, biographer, essayist, and translator, Mqhayi has done more than any other writer to reveal the beauty of Xhosa. He dominated the Xhosa literary field until his death in 1945 and for many years was the model for everybody who tried to write in the language.

The publication of Rubusana's anthology marks the end of the first fifty years of literary activity amongst the Xhosa-speaking people. It is a volume of 570 pages including a glossary, the latter being necessitated by the large number of traditional praise-poems which occupy nearly half the text.[3] But this anthology does not fully reflect the achievements of the writers of this

[2] See *Africa South,* Vol. 2, No. 1, p. 105.
[3] See *Africa South,* Vol. 2, No. 1, p. 101.

first period. It does not include any of Tiyo Soga's writings, nor does it include some of the best prose that Gqoba originally contributed to *Isigidimi*. These appear in *Imibengo* (Tit-Bits), another anthology of prose and poetry prepared by W. G. Bennie, grandson of John Bennie, and published by the Lovedale Press as recently as 1936.

Since the main literary diet of the first writers was the Bible and other religious books, it was only natural that most of them should devote their writing to what they considered the most serious things of life. Their published work consists mainly of history, biography, ethnology, didactic verse, and religious hymns. In spite of the great tradition of the heroic praise-poem, even a man of outstanding literary talent like Gqoba seems to have regarded poetry as a medium through which to express one's religious fervour and nothing else. Gqoba is so soaked in history and legend, as his prose writings reveal, that one is puzzled that none of the "moving accidents" he describes with such spirit ever moved him to immortalize some of these great legendary heroes in poetry.

Soga's superior education put him at an advantage over a man like Gqoba, unquestionably more talented than himself. Soga lived in a much larger world of ideas than his contemporaries, and this is reflected in the range of subjects on which he was able to write as well as in the forms. He wrote short stories, essays and hymns, in addition to the translations mentioned earlier. His very first contribution to the first issue of *Indaba* showed clearly that he was going to write to entertain, and all his contributions to this periodical are characterized by sound commonsense blended with wit and humour. His influence became evident in the contributions of some of the younger writers, e.g., his brother Zaze Soga and William Kobe Ntsikana. The latter has a particular liking for anecdotes connected with cattle raids, and his style is most entertaining. Many other prose writers who broke entirely with sermonizing unfortunately wrote anonymously or just gave their initials. Evidently they were known to the readers of those days, but it is extremely difficult to identify them now. Mqhayi, who began to write just before the Anglo-Boer War, really belongs to the second phase, when literacy had spread to the Sotho- and the Zulu-speaking communities, and his place is in a later essay.

The legacy of the first fifty years of Xhosa literary activity is to be respected. If some of our readers are inclined to think that we are over-indulgent when we make this remark, we have only to remind them that these first writers had no written tradition to guide them, no Homer or Sophocles, no Herodotus or Plutarch, no Dante or Pertrarch on whom to model themselves. If we remember this, then we must agree that theirs was no small achievement.

5
The Early Writers

THOUGH a mere handful, the earliest Xhosa writers deserve at least a whole essay to themselves, not only because they were the first Southern Africans ever to express their thoughts in writing, but also because of the socio-historical interest of their subject the life story of their mentor, Ntsikana. These writers were some of Ntsikana's younger disciples who, in accordance with his dying wish, were "never to return to Xhosa life, but to go to the school (mission station) at Gwali". This was the time of the endless wars amongst various sections of the Xhosa people, especially between Ngqika (misnamed Gaika) and his uncle and one-time regent, Ndlambe. The former was regarded as a traitor by all the other sections of the Xhosa for allowing himself to be used against his own people by the white dispossessors. Two commoners, both of them diviners ('witchdoctors'), had profound social influence among the Xhosa at this time. Ntsikana, a one-time adherent of Ndlambe, later of Ngqika and, ultimately, of Christ; and Makhanda or Nxele (the left-handed warrior misnamed 'Makana'), an adherent of Ndlambe. There was rivalry between these two figures, and, since we know the story only from Ntsikana's disciples, Makhanda inevitably suffers. Although some of them wrote on other subjects later on, it must be emphasized that at the beginning none of these disciples set out to write history as such. They all set out to write about their mentor, and the chiefs are mentioned only in so far as their rule affected Ntsikana. But even from the little that is said about them, we get a fairly clear picture of the characters of Ngqika and Ndlambe.

Ntsikana as Depicted by his Disciples

According to his own disciples, Ntsikana, until his conversion, lived and enjoyed his pagan life as fully as any man of his social accomplishments. He was a great composer, singer and dancer, as well as a polygamist, adulterer, and diviner. The story of his conversion is told by his own son, William Kobe Ntsikana:

> On the day that he was called by the Spirit, he had risen early and was leaning leisurely against the poles of his cattle-fold. When the sun rose, one of its rays smote him. Then he was heard calling to a boy who was attending the calves, 'Do you see what I see?' The boy said, "No". Three times he asked him, and still the boy said "No" ... Then he went to a *mdudo* (dance), together with other people. But on this day, when he stood up to dance, the wind arose. At last he sat down. Then later on he stood up again to dance, and again the wind rose. Thereupon he ordered all those of his household to accompany him home. And when he came to the river, he washed off the red ochre. And they wondered what had befallen him. ...

On reaching home, he told them what had befallen him, and also that they must not listen to Nxele, who was misleading the people, but listen to this Thing that had entered him. 'This Thing that has entered me enjoins that we pray, and that all must kneel!' Thereafter he held divine service at all times, and he was wont to put on his kaross of leopard-skins, and read therefrom.

According to Zaze Soga, Ntsikana was in the land of Ndlambe when it became clear that "this Thing had entered him". Zaze Soga writes:

It was the time of Nxele, a diviner, who preached vapour and vain sayings that have never come true up to this day. At one time he was telling the people that he would make the heavens fall on the White warriors during the fighting at *Rhini* (Grahamstown). Ntsikana was at first inclined to believe Nxele, and he even went so far as to pay tribute to him, presenting him a white ox. For it was an established practice in those days that Nxele should receive tributes from all the people. But later on, when Ntsikana discovered that he had been duped like so many others, he demanded his ox back. ... When war began to threaten, Nxele said that the Xhosa warriors would not fight with spears, but would fight by making the heavens fall on the White warriors. Ntsikana contradicted him, saying, 'Never!' ... When these men, Ntsikana and Nxele, opposed each other so, the royal chief Ndlambe gave his ruling, saying, 'Ntsikana had better lie back awhile, and let us listen to Nxele, otherwise one's ears will clash with each other (i.e., Ntsikana's sayings, entering by one ear, would clash with Nxele's, entering by the other). Why doesn't Ntsikana stay near Ngqika for a time?'
And so it was that Ntsikana returned to his own home, among the Ngqikas, and preached to the people, saying, 'See the people being deceived by Makhanda at Ndlambe's. *My* Thing does not tell me so.'

The disciple who gives the fullest account of Ntsikana is Makhaphela Noyi Balfour, son of Ntsikana's leading disciple and successor. Less inclined to romanticism and mysticism than Ntsikana's own son, Makhapela now and again makes a shrewd observation about the social conditions of his boyhood:

Yes, I knew Ntsikana, son of Gaba. . . . He liked to dress well and looked handsome in his kaross, which was made of the skins of male leopards only, and it was in this kaross that the great one used to preach. . . . Ntsikana founded his school at Mankazana, and it was there that my father Noyi was converted. . . .

It was clear to his disciples that he represented them before God. For the Xhosa people, who were used to diviners, it was easy to conceive of such a thing. Ntsikana had it in him to make his disciples feel the greatness and nearness of God. . . .

At divine service he used to sit near the doorway, while the rest of the hut was filled completely with people, men and women. His kaross of male leopard skins covered his body entirely, that body that he would not reveal even to himself.

The prelude to the service was the hymn, *That Great Cloak That Covereth Us.* And when his disciples had thus acknowledged his entry, he would then preach this Thing that had entered him, this Thing that hated sin. And he would name what was sinful in their daily lives, pointing out whatever in them was hateful to God . . . This man preached Christ, saying, 'Repent ye! Repent ye from your sins!' He preached the Son of God, the only begotten of His Father, the Great Cloak, the true Refuge, the Stronghold and Rock of Truth. . . .

Ntsikana was wont to describe the man Dafeti (David), proclaiming him the great progenitor of all Believers. The names of Adam, Dafeti and the coming Mesiyasi (Messiah) we first heard from Ntsikana . . . . Be it always known that among the Xhosa of old, God produced the prophet Ntsikana, who had no learning at all, in a manner that was dim and vague at the time, but which has become bright and clear in our own days . . . .

On Ntsikana's preaching, his people accepted this Thing, even though they did not tumble over one another in going into it, considering how eagerly he was urging them .... Ngqika was the first to accept it. He said: 'In order that the Thing may be acceptable, I had better be the first to join it'. But because he adhered so much to this outmoded Xhosa way of life, he was easily led away from his aim by his councillors.

For a long time after being 'led away' by his pagan councillors, however, Ngqika continued to have faith in Ntsikana and his strategy in war. It was an ill-fated military expedition against Ndlambe, in which Ntsikana's divination took too long to foresee "the gnats swarming on the skulls" of Ngqika's dead warriors, that decided the issue for the army commanders. And on their return, the latter clamoured that "these praying men" be killed. "How can we be defeated when they are praying?" they asked angrily.

It was after this disastrous campaign that Ntsikana and some of his leading disciples had to flee for their lives. Makhaphela Noyi Balfour makes mention of 'the flight to Tambo': "Wherever we stopped for the night, we boys, in accordance with Ntsikana's orders, had to make a large clearing in the bush, trim it and make it beautiful, in order to raise a place of worship .... We kept this up throughout the flight, and never were we without a structure in which to worship our Great Creator".

The last days of Ntsikana are described by Kobe and Makhaphela. According to both writers, Ntsikana had his grave dug and his coffin made of *mhlunguthi* some time before his death. And every now and then, he would lie in the coffin and have it lowered into the grave, to make sure that everything would go smoothly when the time came. According to Kobe, Ntsikana's relatives used to weep when he did this. Whereupon he would say, "I was only your light. No messenger goes on a mission never to return. I was only a messenger".

One day after they (the senior disciples) had lowered him into the grave, he said jokingly, "You might as well throw in the soil". For he was a great joker. "Hear the *mfundisi* ordering us" exclaimed Noyi. But Matshaya said "Never! Even a homeless wanderer must be quite dead and still before his body can be covered with soil". So they helped him out of the grave. But on a certain night, towards the coming of dawn, the spirit of the prophet departed.

Alas! The wailings that were to be heard! ... They have never ceased ringing in my ears .... It was as if even the cliffs and forests had joined in the wailing! He was buried by Noyi and Matshaya with great ceremony. His coffin was fastened with thongs made from ox-hide, not nailed as we do nowadays.

And so the famous son of Gaba slept in the cold ground just at the age of real manhood.

After Ntsikana's Death

The story is carried beyond Ntsikana's death by the writers we have already quoted and by other contemporaries. Makhaphela writes:

Some of these disciples of the son of Gaba were baptized by the first White missionaries and given more training in the Truth that they had accepted .... Each person was given a new name by which he would be known as a Christian. So it was that Noyi (Makhaphela's own father) was renamed 'Balfour'. This became the practice for us who had chosen this new road. Nonetheless it was strange, because we had never seen anything wrong with our own names. But so eagerly was this new teaching accepted that many a man, even while still a pagan, kept in mind some new name that he fancied, so that, in the event of his becoming a Christian, he should be known by that name.

This explains such names as William and Balfour, which make such very strange reading in this context.

Ntsikana's disciples were always watchful lest the teachings of missionaries should clash with what they had themselves been taught. John Muir Vimbe writes: "I am thankful that the Maker-of-all-things has preserved me until I even saw His Word written in our own tongue . . . . This Word too regards as evil those things that we have always regarded as evil: theft, adultery, killing, lying and many other abominations as enumerated in Leviticus xviii, 6–30".

The name of Satan, which they first got to know from the missionaries, did not clash with Ntsikana's teaching, for his disciples accepted it immediately and associated it with all the things that looked ugly to them. Says Zaze Soga: "In their prayers they used to say that all those things that were pleasing to the eye were from God, and all the ugly ones from Satan. So it was that they were wont to say in their prayers, 'Thou God Who art in Heaven! Most Beautiful! Creator of birds and beasts (all the beautiful ones being named), unlike Satan who, in trying to create birds, produced the bat and the owl.' "

Ntsikana's Place in African Life and Literature

It is unfortunate that, due to the universal human weakness for 'miracles', latter-day zealots have disregarded verifiable historical facts and all but deified Ntsikana. We cannot blame Kobe for recording his father's religious experiences as told to him. After all, when his father was 'called by the Spirit', Kobe was

only a child and could not have been present at the
festivities where the rising wind was supposed to have
forbidden Ntsikana to dance. The same Kobe records
that 'Nyhengane' (Dr. van der Kemp) preached among
the Xhosa people, and that Ntsikana's contemporary
and rival, Makhanda, who preached the 'resurrection
of the dead' and condemned witchcraft and adultery,
declared openly that he was a follower of 'Nyhegane'.
There can be no doubt that Ntsikana, who was so
closely associated with the chiefs who gave 'Nyhengane' permission to preach, must have heard this man
preach and read from 'the Book'. Yet the zealots want
to believe that the names and stories of Adam, David
and the Messiah were communicated to Ntsikana 'directly from God'. Again, in spite of the mission at
Gwali, where Ntsikana enjoined his disciples to go after
his death, the zealots assert that Ntsikana never saw a
white man, but 'prophesied' the coming of 'a people
with flowing hair'. Kobe records also that, when
Ngqika made it known that he was going to seek the
help of *amaNgesi* (English soldiers) against Ndlambe, it
was Ntsikana who warned him that if he did so, the
land of the Xhosa people would be the booty of the
white man. Again, it was during Ntsikana's life-time
that Makhanda succeeded in uniting the Ngqikas and
the Ndlambes in order to raid Grahamstown. This was
in 1819. Ntsikana's biographers tell us that he died in
1821, that is, two years after Makhanda, who was
drowned in his attempt to escape from captivity on
Robben Island.

The importance of Ntsikana lies not in the legendary
smitings by the shafts of sunrise, nor in the rising
winds and readings from karosses. The fact that his

Hymn of Praise is the first literary composition ever to be assigned to individual formulation—thus constituting a bridge between the traditional and the post-traditional period—is of great historical significance. But even more important than this is the fact that, through his influence, a few young disciples were introduced to the arts of reading and writing, and that, inspired by his exemplary life and teaching, these men became the harbingers of the dawn of literacy amongst the indigenous peoples of Southern Africa.

6
Literary Stabilization

THE period immediately succeeding that of Ntsikana's disciples may be regarded as one of literary stabilization amongst the Xhosa-speaking Southern Africans. The Bible had been translated into Xhosa and Tiyo Soga, one of its translators, had also translated *The Pilgrim's Progress* (Part I). These two books had profound influence on the thought and style of the writers. The idea of individual, as against communal, formulation had taken root, but writers did not abandon the traditional style in their expression, nor did they cast aside their folklore. New experiments in versification began to appear, but the traditional forms asserted themselves all the time. It must be remembered that this was a transitional period in every detail of the people's lives. While the missionary carried on his work as preacher and teacher, the soldier carried on with his own mission of conquest. While the missionary preached "peace on earth and goodwill towards men," the wars of dispossession were working towards a climax. The people had seen the disastrous effects of the Nongqawuse (Cattle-killing) Episode, which had impoverished them and driven thousands of their sons and daughters to seek work amongst their white conquerors; and the effects of the master-and-servant relationship between white and black were beginning to be keenly felt. Those who had accepted the teachings of the missionaries were no longer blindly optimistic about the motives of the white man. All this, and more, is reflected in the writings of the sixties to eighties of the last century.

The dominant figures of this period were Tiyo Soga, who wrote essays and a few short stories, and William W. Gqoba, essayist, historian, and poet. The novel was not yet born. Imitations of *The Pilgrim's Progress* were to come with the next generation.

Prose

The essay of this period was not unlike the English essay of the eighteenth century in content. It was serious and didactic. Soga's essays reflect the social changes of the time very clearly. He writes under such headings as 'Amakristu Neenkosi' (The Christians and the Chiefs), 'Amakhoiwa Namaqaba' (The Believers and the Pagans). The former opens as follows: "It is said by outsiders that as soon as people follow the ways of the Word of God, they no longer pay regard to the earthly chieftainship and its authority. It is said that if a chief or other man of standing finds himself amongst the converted, he is lost, for he enjoys no recognition as a chief or man of standing. And so these outsiders, who still hold out stubbornly against the Word, go on to say, 'As for us, we still stand by the chiefs and the sons of the chiefs who have been deserted by their people, by those people who have accepted the way of God'." The writer goes on to say that the chiefs themselves have become so very much aware of this attitude on the part of the Christians that "as far as they are concerned, the Christians are a separate flock, a different tribe, that has nothing to do with them." The writer deplores this state of affairs, and warns his Christian readers that if the pagans are to be attracted to Christianity, the converted must never be accused of lack of respect for their chiefs. He quotes a great deal from the Scriptures to establish his point that "God recognizes earthly power. It exists at His bequest. And he who rejects the chiefs, rejects God's own bequest."

The essay on 'The Believers and the Pagans' also shows that the gulf is widening between the converted and the pagan. The converted has lost *ubuntu* (generosity, respect for man irrespective of position). The pagan can no longer expect hospitality amongst the Christians. Soga gives an instance of a pagan traveller who spent a cold night in the open veld because none of the Christians in the village would admit him into their homes. Another essay of this type by the same writer describes the devastating effects of the White man's liquor:

White people brought us knowledge and wisdom in respect of many things. If we were willing that our young people should partake of that wealth of knowledge and wisdom, we should be lifted out of ignorance. For to the white people too, this wisdom and knowledge is not indigenous. It came at a certain time. There was a time when their progenitors were the laughing stock of their more civilized conquerors. Today, the white people laugh at us.

More than anything else, it was through the white people that we got to know about God, about Jesus, about freedom and about heaven. But although they have brought many things that are blessings to us in this life and even in the life hereafter, there are some evil things which we wish that the white people had left behind. Even the blessings have lost their value and can no longer be praised as blessings, if we look at the work done by liquor amongst the black people. Liquor has produced abominations which were not known amongst the Xhosa people, abominations that we cannot discuss now. Liquor is going to destroy, whereas the other things came to uplift us. Liquor is like a firebrand thrown into dry veld grass.

Other essayists of this time dealt with similar subjects. Witchcraft, or belief in 'diviners', is tackled from all angles by several essayists, and all of them, of course, think that superstition is incompatible with 'true Christianity'.

But it must not be thought that the essayists of this period never wrote for entertainment. Soga, even in those essays referred to above, is very humorous. It is only a pity that most of the time he addresses himself to a Christian audience, so that a great deal of what he has to say would receive no sympathy from the pagans whom he himself refers to as 'outsiders'. In what perhaps is the greatest essay that has yet been published in Xhosa, Soga describes a journey by ox-waggon through a drought-stricken area in the Eastern Province. It is a ghastly picture of hunger and desolation. But even in this the man's deep sense of humour occasionally reveals itself, throwing into relief the barren journey between King William's Town and Adelaide.

Far more entertaining than the essay of this period is the short story, though only a few examples of it are to be found. The leading figure here is Kobe Ntsikana, son of the prophet. He deals mostly with scenes from pastoral life. But one of the greatest entertainers and humorists of this period is anonymous. The following is a sample of his writing:

One day, while riding my father's horse, Stanley, I decided when passing near the great pond on the road-side to give the horse a slight thwack on the flank, in order that by the time I came in sight of the homesteads near the school, all the eyes of the village should be upon me, because I had an eye on someone fair in that village. But Stanley, instead of ambling gracefully as I had intended he should, got completely out of control and made straight for the pond. And the pond was full to overflowing! Imagine me sitting there on his back, a heap of death. But just when he reached the brink, Stanley suddenly stopped. I tell you I flew right over his head and went splash! into the pond, sinking, and finally sat right on the mud at the bottom.

Sitting down there, I began to think hard, realizing that I was as good as dead. I could not even swim, because my leggings were full of water. I was like one who had been bound to a heavy stone and cast into the water. Nevertheless, I began to struggle, remembering that God helps those who help themselves. But in vain! I could not move from the spot . . . .

Then suddenly I caught hold of my hair and pulled it hard, and I realized that my body was rising. Ah! Now I remembered that bodies lose weight in water, so I pulled in earnest. Lo and behold! My body rose easily, and I pulled and threw myself right out of the water and onto the brink!

And so the story continues in this humorous manner. The first person to see the narrator in his sad plight, covered with mud and all but dead, was the very schoolmistress whom he had hoped to attract from Stanley's back! But the story, of course, ends happily.

Poetry

Apart from one or two lyrical poems, the poetry of this period is didactic. The titles themselves indicate the subject matter—"The Song of the Cross", "Isaiah I", "Acts 28". Then there are Gqoba's long poems on Education and Christianity.

But while the literary poets were experimenting with new themes and new forms of versification, the tribal bards who stood by the chiefs and the sons of the chiefs carried on with their compositions in the traditional style. It is most interesting to see this transitional period from the literary as well as from the social point of view, through the eyes of the Christian literary poet on the one hand, and through the eyes of the tribal bard on the other. Towards the end of this period we also find that some poets live fully in both worlds. It will be necessary to deal separately with the poetry of this period.

7
Reaction to Conquest

THE African tribal bard sees life mainly through the social institutions of his own tribe. The Christian literary poet sees it partly through the tribal institutions and partly through the institutions introduced by the white missionary and by the white administrator. To understand the early literary poet amongst the Xhosa, we must put him side by side with the traditional tribal bard of the same period.

The Tribal Bard and the New Order

It must be repeated that the African traditional praise-poem is not, as most white people think, just a song of praise in which the bard showers flattering epithets on his chief. (See *Africa South,* Vol. 2, No. 1, Oct./Dec. 1957.) The "praises of the chiefs" deal primarily with the happenings in and around the tribe during the reign of a given chief, praising what is worthy and decrying

what is unworthy, and even forecasting what is going
to happen: rivalries for the chieftainship within the
tribe; the ordinary social life; alliances and conflicts
with neighbouring tribes; military and political triumphs and reverses, etc. Thus the African bard is a
chronicler as well as being a poet. The chief is only the
center of the praise-poem because he is the symbol of
the tribe as a whole.

This period being that of "treatises", annexations,
and "resettlements", we are able to see, through the
eyes of the African bard, the encroachment of the
white man on the land of the Africans, the breaking of
alliances between one tribe and another, boundary dis-
putes, the undermining of the power of the chief by
missionary and magistrate, the relations between non-
Christian and Christian, etc.

As the Xhosa people were the first to be subjugated,
it is in the "praises" of their chiefs that the vast social
changes brought about by conquest are first reflected.
Most of our illustrations refer to this group.

The "praises" composed in the middle of the nineteenth century and after, begin to make allusions to
governors, missionaries and magistrates. In the "praises
of Sandile" (son of Ngqika or Gaika), reference is made
to Smiti (Sir Harry Smith), who was governor when
Sandile was arrested and sent to Rini (Grahamstown)
via Monti (East London). Reference is also made to
Kondile (Rev. Henry Calderwood) and to Tshalisi (the
Hon. Charles Brownlee) who became magistrates over
the Ngqika section of the Xhosa after their conquest.
John Henderson Soga (son of Tiyo Soga) regards
Brownlee as "a friend of the Bantu" (see "The South
Eastern Bantu", chapter XV), but the Ngqika tribal

bard of the days of Brownlee thinks otherwise. He complains that "the land has been spoilt by the Calderwoods" and that "we trust not Tshalisi who seems to be friends with the Germans". He also refers sarcastically to the "guardianship" of Charles Brownlee over Sandile, so choosing his words that the "guardianship" looks like the herding of a domestic animal by its master.

In the "praises of Sarhili" reference is made to the exile of this chief, and to his finding sanctuary among the Bomvana. The relationship between his people and the Fingo buffer-state are also evident. But Sarhili himself is not spared. The war that led to his exile started as a mere drunken brawl between some Xhosa men and their Fingo neighbours. Handled properly, the quarrel could have been settled in a local headman's court. But Sarhili was led to treat the "breaking of Mbune's pots" which led to the fight, as a casus belli. The bard refers sarcastically to this:

Alas! that the land should die for Mbune's pots!

In this and many other poems, constant reference is made to the role of the fugitive Fingos who, having been "taken under his wing" by the Xhosa chief, deserted him and made friends with "their fathers, the white men". Always the Fingo are reminded that their place is with the other blacks, and their attention is drawn to the kind of things that have been done to them. Thus, in the "praises of Ngangelizwe" (a Thembu chief), the Bhele clan are asked:

... what cause have ye to complain?
We gave you the Mthentu rich in corn.

There does not seem to be any direct bitterness towards the missionaries. But the African Christians are often subjected to sarcasm. Their divided loyalty, even as individuals, often provoked whippings, if not contemptuous amusement. It was the summary manner in which he used to deal with defiant Christians that earned the Mpondomise chief, Mhlontlo, the epithet of "Wader-with-the-sjambok-among-the-Christians".

The "praises of Dalindyebo", son of Ngangelizwe and his successor, refer to the Christians' love for "the song":

> Which they sing in praise of the King,
> Proclaiming Jehovah and Christ:
> How strange to us that they turn to Him their
>   buttocks,
> Albeit proclaiming Him King.

The Xhosa bards are painfully aware of the havoc wrought by the white man's liquor amongst the displaced and perplexed chiefs. Ndimba, grandson of Ndlambe, was ejected by Makeleni (Col. McLean) from his rightful home, and came to live in Charles Brownlee's magisterial district where he apparently received an allowance of some kind. This he spent on liquor in a canteen owned by one Kelly at Draaibosch:

> He helplessly lives in the House of Tshalisi
> Whom he loves for paying a wage;
> This child may be found in Keli's canteen,
> Bearing patiently the kicks of the German.

But most tragic of all in this respect is reference to Maqoma. A great warrior and orator, the hero of the Battle of Mthontsi (War of Mlanjeni 1852), a regent

with a keen sense of justice, Maqoma after his defeat
bore himself with such dignity at the rough handling
of Sir Harry Smith as to shame this arrogant soldier-
governor. But, before he was banished to Robben Island where he met his death, he had so succumbed to
liquor that the anonymous bard, while giving him genuine praise for his exploits, also refers to him as one
"whose tracks are strewn with broken bottles".

The Early Literary Poets

The Christian African found a new meaning in life. He
fully accepted the new culture with its promise of a
fullness of life. The way to this promised life went by
way of the baptismal font, the church and the school.
These were incompatible with tribal life and its institutions, and so at this period the Christian African is at
the cross-roads. To the semi-literate one, the new road,
though preferable, is misty. He is not so far removed
from the old ways as not to be attracted by them. The
intellectual has a clearer understanding of both roads.
He prefers the new, but is keenly aware of the changing
attitude of the conquerer. The fullness of life that was
promised him is not to be realized in the foreseeable
future.

On the other hand, he regards the tribal institutions
as backward and only serving to delay this fullness of
life for himself and his people. His aspirations and his
feeling of frustration are to be seen through the eyes of
the poet of this period. (The influence of Christian
teaching is evident everywhere.)

William W. Gqoba

In the field of verse, Gqoba is famous for his two "Great Discussions", one between the Christian and Non-Christian, and the other on Education. The names of the participants in these discussions, show the influence of Tiyo Soga's translation of *The Pilgrim's Progress,* in that they are symbolic. In the discussion between the Christian and the non-Christian, there are two participants, namely, *Present-world* (non-Christian) and *World-to-come* (Christian). They discuss matters related to the world, matters related to education, to social life, and to government.

Present-world praises the earth and its pleasures and richness of life, so rich that even the Christians look this way and that, and finally join the ranks of the non-Christians who openly and joyfully welcome everything that life can give. He enumerates the pastimes of the non-Christians. He alleges that if the Christians were truthful, they would admit that they, in fact, had lost their faith. Their youth are drunkards. Meanwhile, the white man in whose favour the Christians abandoned their chiefs, made no difference between the Christians and the non-Christians. He (white man) subjected them all to the same laws. All things considered, the life of the non-Christian was much fuller and richer because, while, in addition to present-world self-denial and sufferings, the Christians still feared to go to hell after death; the non-Christian looked forward to a peaceful and becoming life with his fathers in the land of the shades.

You deserted your chiefs and came to the
    Whiteman;

You destroyed our rule and sided with the enemy;
But now your faith is lean and shrivell'd
Even like a chameleon whose mouth is smear'd
With nicotine on a sultry summer's day.

World-to-come replies. He reminds his interlocutor
that Ntsikana said that from the East there would come
the claypot of corn beer (brought by the Fingos), and
from the West the "little barrel" brought by the white
man: that these two would bring misfortune. But how
could Present-world talk of "the pleasures of this life"?
What did they amount to? What was the end of those
who aimed at riches? In life were they any happier than
their poorer brethren? Did they not suffer from disease? Did they not lose their loved ones by death? At
death were they any happier?

> Why boast you of sin
> That stalks man to the grave?
> Will you stay a sinner,
> Like a locust that dies
> On a dry stalk of grass?

The discussion covers 900 lines. In it Gqoba shows
his knowledge of history and folklore. The participants
refer to numerous incidents in history and now and
again a folktale is told to illustrate a point. Present-
world has a very strong case throughout, but somehow
at the end he gives in.

The participants in the Great Discussion on Education are youthful people of both sexes. They include
such characters as Sharp-eyed, Crooked-eyed, One-
sided, Miss Vagrant, Miss Gossip, Miss Truthful, and
Miss Upright. They are critical of the educational practice of the day. They are denied access to certain fields

of knowledge; they are poorly paid. There is a conspir-
acy among the rulers, and it is this: "If they cry for
Greek and Latin and Hebrew, give them a little. But
make no mistake about the wages. Keep the wages low.
If they are employed in respectable jobs, flatter them by
addressing them as "Mr. So-and-So", but as ordinary
labourers they are to be addressed as plain "Jack" or
just "Boy!"

But the inevitable "moderates" are to be found even
in this small group. Accusing the first group of being
"ungrateful" and of "finding fault with everything",
they warn them not to expect to get everything at once.
They must expect to take just as long to acquire civilization as the white people. After all, hadn't the white
people brought them happiness?

While the lion of darkness still roared and roared,
They gave up their homeland for love of us Blacks.

A participant by the name of Tactless confesses to
disillusionment. We thought, he says, that this way of
life was going to be a refuge for those who had been
smelt out as sorcerers, for suffering womanhood, for
young children who had none to protect them. For
these and many other blessings we gave up our independence. But now the main thing is taxes; a tax on
firewood, a tax on water, a tax on grass even. We are
deprived of our pastureland. In good faith, we allowed
white traders to come and live among us, sharing our
pastures with us. Today the land belongs to them. If
our cattle go anywhere near, they are impounded. Nevertheless, says, Tactless, we must admit that the white
man's things are good. We must get them, no matter
how much pain this costs us. If you want honey, you

thrust your hand and grab it no matter how vicious the bees; no matter how painful the stings.

There is an interesting variety of participants and therefore a variety of opinions, left, centre and right, shading into each other. In this long discussion, no one says that the blacks are getting a square deal from the whites. The best defense that the extreme right can put up is that things are not so bad, and that if the ingrates will only exercise patience, the best is yet to be. The last speaker is Ungrateful, who admits that his eyes "have been opened" to the "good things" that the white man brought them, and brings the Great Discussion that covers 1800 lines to a close by telling the participants to "go seek learning" and "love the White people".

Smaller in quantity but decidedly greater in quality is H. M. Mthakathi's *Song of the Cross*. A poem of 200 lines, it calls upon the "Bringer-together-of homes, whose blood didst flow whilst Thou didst hunt for our souls" to "proclaim the news of heaven in the rough places of the earth". He thinks of the great upheavals in his homeland, of the thousands whose bones lie scattered at Mthombe and Sandlwana, and prays that these may dance at the gates of Zion. He prays that the Lord reveal Himself to the youth:

Reveal Thyself to the youth of our land,
That they give up the song and dance,
And go arm in arm to the places of learning,
And go arm in arm to the praise of the Highest.

Such is Mthakathi's prayer to the Christ,

Whose shoulders bore the cross of shame
That the pagan might wear a crown.

Mthakathi speaks from the heart; Gqoba, on the other hand, is forced by the very manner in which he handles his subject matter to speak from the head. In the latter's two great poems, there is more wit than emotion. But both of these, the greatest poets of the period, preserve the imagery that characterizes the traditional praise-poem, as well as showing the influence of the new learning not only in subject matter, but also in technique.

8

The Tale of Nongqawuse

NONGQAWUSE is the name of the girl generally held responsible for the "National Suicide of the
Xhosa People" in 1856–1857. The story of her meeting
with the "spirits of warriors long dead", of their enjoin-
ing her to tell chiefs and the people to destroy all their
livestock and food stores, of the carrying out of this
injunction, and of the subsequent famine and deaths,
all this is told in records of missionaries and colonial
officials, who were working amongst the Xhosa when
these things happened. And all those who are familiar
with South African history know it either directly from
these records or from ordinary history books. Yet very
few people know that there is an account of this incident, written by an African who was living at the time,
to be found in Rubusana's Anthology, "Zemk' Iinkomo
Magwala ndini", and that the author is no other than
William W. Gqoba, the historian-poet who has figured
so often already in this series.

Gqoba was born in 1840, so that at the climax of this calamity he was seventeen years old. At that age, a boy in African primitive society has many social obligations and responsibilities, and though he may not be a direct participant in tribal councils, he is very well informed as to what takes place there. With its details of people's names, clan and place-names, Gqoba's account sounds very authentic, and for this reason we propose to give a faithful translation of its Xhosa original, as the finest of the renderings of a story that still lives in the emotions and thoughts of the Xhosa people today. We adhere to his own spelling of the Xhosa names, many of which are well-known surnames at the present time, spelt as they were spelt by him.

The Cause of the Cattle-Killing at the Nongqawuse Period
By: W. W. G.

It so happened that in the Thenjini region of Gcalekaland, in the ward of headman Mnzabele, in the year 1856, two girls went out to the lands to keep the birds away from the corn. One was named Nongqawuse, daughter of Mhlakaza, and the other the daughter of a sister of Mhlakaza's. Near a river known as the Kamanga two men approached them and said, "Convey our greetings to your people, and tell them we are So-and-So and So-and-So" (giving their names). And the names by which they called themselves turned out to be the names of people who were known to have died long ago. They went on to say: "You are to tell the people that the whole community is about to rise again from the dead. Then go on to say to them all the cattle living now must be slaughtered, for they are reared with defiled hands, as the people handle witchcraft. Say to them there must be no ploughing of lands, rather must the people dig deep pits (granaries), erect new huts, set up wide, strongly built cattlefolds, make milk-sacks, and weave doors from buka roots. The people must give up witchcraft on their own, not waiting until they are exposed by the witchdoctors. You are to tell them that these are the words of their chiefs, —the words of Napakade (Forever), the son of Sifubasibanzi (the Broad-chested).

On reaching home the girls reported this, but no one would listen to them. Everybody ridiculed them instead. On the following day, they went again to keep the birds away from the corn, and after some time, these men appeared again and asked if the girls had told the people at home, and what the people had said in reply. The girls reported that their message had simply been a thing of laughter, no one believing them. "The people simply said we were telling stories". This happened in Gcalekaland near the mouth of the Gxara.

The men then said: "Say to the elders that they are to call all the chiefs together from Gcaleka's, Tato's, Ngqika's and from the Gqunukhwebe, and they must tell the news to them".

On the following morning, Mhlakaza and some other men went to the lands, but these strangers did not reveal themselves. They were heard without being seen. It was only Nongqawuse and the other girl who heard them, and it was Nongqawuse who interpreted what was being said by the spirits. They said: "Tell those men to go and call the chiefs and bring them here. Only then shall we reveal ourselves".

Some men then went to Rili's royal place at Hohita, and there the strange news was related by Mhlakaza's daughter. Then Rili sent out Botomani, a minor chief, to go and verify this thing. Botomani went, but the strangers did not reveal themselves. Then Rili sent messengers to tell the chiefs that there were people who had been heard by Mhlakaza's daughter to say all the chiefs must be called together to meet the chief Napakade, son of Sifubasibanzi, near the mouth of the Gxara.

From Tato's came Maramnco, son of Fadana, accompanied by Shele, son of Zizi. From the Ndungwane came Dulaze, son of Qwesha, related to Ndarala. From the Tshatshus came Mpeke, son of Mfeneni. From the Ngqika came Namba, great son of Maqoma. From the Gcaleka section came Rili and Lindinxiwa, sons of Hintsa, together with Ngubo, son of Mlashe, and Nxiti, son of Lutshaba. From the Ndlambes came Nowawe, son of Ndlambe. From the Gqunukwebe came Dilima, son of Pato. All these men made their way to the home of Mhlakaza near the Gxara.

On arriving there, they were told that Nongqawuse desired that the numbers to go to the Gxara be reduced, and that those who were to go must be mostly chiefs. This in truth was done.

As the people were rather fearful, it happened that as they drew near the River Kamango, their throats went dry, and they felt thirsty. Meanwhile Nongqawuse, beautifully painted with red ochre, led the way. Then those who were thirsty were heard to say: "Is one who is thirsty allowed to drink?"

Nongqawuse replied, "He who does not practice witchcraft may drink without fear".

Thereupon Dilima, hero son of Pato, removed his kaross and stooped to drink. Then one by one the other men of Nomagwayi wase Mbo followed suit.

The Vision

Just at this time, there was a tremendous crash of big boulders breaking loose from the cliffs overlooking the headwaters of the River Kamanga, whereupon, the men gazed at one another wondering, for they were seized with fear. It seemed that some unknown thing on the cliffs was going to burst into flames.

While they stood wondering, the girl was heard saying, "Just cast your eyes in the direction of the sea".

And when they looked intently at the waters of the sea, it seemed as if there were people there in truth, and there were sounds of bulls bellowing, and oxen too. There was a huge formless black object that came and went, came and went and finally vanished over the crests of the waves of the sea.

Then it was that all the people began to believe.

The army in the sea never came out to meet the chiefs, and even what they said was not heard by any besides Nongqawuse. After it had vanished, she said: "The Chiefs yonder say you are to return to your homes and slaughter àll your cattle and, in order that the resurrection may hasten, you are not to rear any cattle. You are not to plough the fields, but make big new pits (granaries), and these you will suddenly find full of corn. Erect new huts and make many doors. Shut yourselves in your huts, because on the eight day, when the community returns in the company of Napa-kade, son of Sifubasibanzi, all the beasts on the land and in the rivers, and all the snakes will be roaming the land. You are also to take out all the old corn in the pits and throw it away. In order to survive, you are to use many doors to close each hut, fasten every door tightly, and abstain from witchcraft".

She went on to say that there was another chief, mounted on a grey horse. His name was Grey, either-wise known as Satan. All those who did not slaughter their cattle would become the subjects of the chief named Satan, and such people would not see the glory of our own chief, Napakade, son of Sifubasibanzi.

That then was the cause of the cattle-killing of 1856 to 1857.

In the midst of this there appeared another young girl from the house of Nkwitshi of the Kwemta clan, in the Ndlambe section near the Mpongo. Her name was Nonkosi. The message of this girl was one with Nong-qawuse's. She used to lead the people to a pond there at the Mpongo, and there used to see abakweta dancing on the surface of the water, and they thought that they heard the thudding of the oxhide, accompanied by a song, to which the abakweta danced. Truly, the people were so deluded that they went so far as to claim that they had seen the horns of cattle, heard the lowing of milk-cows, the barking of dogs, and the songs of milk-men at milking time.

The Orders of the Chiefs

On reaching their homes, the chiefs assembled their subjects and made known the news of the ancestors who were expected to return to life, fresh and strong, of the promised coming-to-life again of the cattle they were about to slaughter and of those that they had slaughtered long ago.

Nongqawuse had said that anyone who, on slaughtering his ox, decided to dispose of its carcass by barter, should nevertheless engage its soul, in order that on its coming back to life it should be his property. And she had said that all those who did not slaughter their cattle would be carried by a fierce hurricane and thrown into the sea to drown and die.

The community was split in two. One section believed that the resurrection of the people would come some day, but not that of the cattle. Thereupon, father fell out with son, brother with brother, chief with subjects, relative with relative. Two names emerged to distinguish the two groups. One group was named amaTamba (the Submissive), that is, Nongqawuse's converts. The other was called amaGogotya (the Unyielding), that is, those who were stubborn and would not kill their cattle. So some slaughtered their cattle, and others did not.

The Eighth Day

As the killing of the cattle went on, those who had slaughtered hurriedly for fear of being smelt out began to starve and had to live by stealing the livestock of others. Then everybody looked forward to the eighth day. It was the day on which the sun was expected to rise red, and to set again in the sky. Then there would follow great darkness, during which the people would shut themselves in their huts. Then the dead would rise and return to their homes, and then the light of day would come again.

On that day the sun rose as usual. Some people washed their eyes with sea-water at the mouth of the Buffalo. Some peered outside through little apertures in their huts, while those who had never believed went about their daily outdoor tasks. Nothing happened. The sun did not set, no dead person came back to life, and not one of the things that had been predicted came to pass.

Such then was the Nongqawuse catastrophe. The people died of hunger and disease in large numbers. Thus it was that whenever thereafter a person said an unbelievable thing, those who heard him, said: "You are telling a Nongqawuse tale".

9

Land, Labour, Literature

THE Xhosa prose and verse writings of the last thirty years of the nineteenth century provide a wealth of material not only on the intellectual and literary development of the African peoples, but also on the drastic political, economic and social changes affecting all groups in Southern Africa.

The Nongqawuse cattle-killing episode had broken the economic independence of the Xhosa, hunger and poverty driving them in large numbers into the colony to earn a livelihood as labourers. Though not yet subdued, the Xhosa chiefs had lost their political and military power. Some of their people, e.g., a section of the Ndlambe and almost the entire Gqunukwowebe, had become Christian. From these and the "loyal Fingos" there developed not only a class of preachers and teachers, but also a kind of "police tribe", whom the Colonial Government moved into the tracts of land depopulated by the famine and pestilence that had resulted from the cattle-killing. Fingos and other tribal groups displaced by the internecine Mfecane Wars were pushed away from the Colony and into the "empty spaces" and "no-man's-lands" immediately bordering upon unconquered territories and the annexed territories that could not yet be "trusted". Together with the descendants of Ntsikana's disciples and the white missionaries, they carried the "Word" and literacy to these areas. But also they acted as the "ears of the Government", and they "set the example to the backward peoples" by encouraging their sons to go and work in the industrial centres. For this was a period of industrial expansion, and there was a desperate need for labour in the mining industry and its concomitants, like the railways. The Trek Boers were involved in a life-and-death struggle with the indigenous peoples, especially in the Transvaal with the Pedi people under their chief, Sekhukhuni. Everywhere there was unrest, because the shortage of labour necessitated the acceleration of the Wars of Dispossession, in order that all the "able-bodied men" could be squeezed out of the tribal territories and into the labour market. Labour-recruiting Native Commissioners were no less active than the missionaries in the "backward areas", and there was a positive scramble for converts among the church bodies. Literacy was developing in quality as well as in quantity; and all this constitutes the subject matter of the literature during the last thirty years of the nineteenth century.

By 1870, the stage was set for the last phase of the Wars of Dispossession. The writers of the period have a great deal to say about events they were living through, but what we are most grateful for is the unconscious co-operation between them and the tribal bards. The intellectuals write straightforward narratives, and the tribal bards compose and recite praise-poems in the traditional manner, often making references in figurative language to the incidents narrated by the intellectuals. In this way, much that would otherwise be obscure in the traditional praise-poem is elucidated by the straightforward historical record. Here we can only indicate briefly the nature of this co-operation:

1. The intellectual writes that, as a result of starvation, the victims of the Nongqawuse fraud have become homeless wanderers, out of touch with any form of tradition, because the white employer does not really accept them into his society. The tribal bard says:

> Nongqawuse created the homeless squatters;
> Can it be that she spoke the truth?
> Slaughter your cattle! But save the dogs,
> For plenty of game is coming!

2. The intellectual describes the mass removals of "police tribes" to fill the "empty spaces". The tribal bard says:

> He has made the Fingos defiant,
> Depriving us of land and power.
> See how they stretch from Cwecweni to Ngquthu,
> How they turn Phalo's land upside down!

3. In the general rising of 1880–1881, when the African tribes protested against the Act of Disarmament, the followers of the Mpondomise chief, Mhlontlo, killed the Qumbu magistrate or "Resident", Anthony Hope, and then tried to break through to Basutoland to make common cause with the Basotho then engaged in

the Gun War. But they were held up by the "loyal
Hlubi" under their chief Zibi, until the colonial troops
and their black allies came and defeated Mhlontlo. The
tribal bard says of Zibi:

> He is the Foiler of the mighty elephant,
> For he foiled Mhlontlo and returned unscathed.

4. Mhlontlo, however, managed to escape, and was
for a long time in hiding while the red-coats sought
high and low for him. The tribal bard says:

> The red-coats throng the Tsitsa Falls,
> Awaiting the return of Mhlontlo
> Whose name is loathsome to the whites,
> For he killed the Resident Hope.

5. Finally Mhlontlo eluded the red-coats, crossed the
Gqili (Orange River) and reached Basutoland, where he
found sanctuary. Meanwhile the Colony was engaged
in unsuccessful war against the Basotho. The tribal
bard says:

> We espied the trail of Mhlontlo;
> He traversed Silwanyana's and vanished in the Gqili;
> But the land of the Sotho is a stronghold of
>   mountains
> Whence they hurl the spear and the battle-axe,
> Putting the white warriors to flight.

6. When the Mpondo chief, Sigcawu, came to meet
Major Elliott and the Kokstad Resident, Macdonald,
his entourage made a display that was interpreted as an
act of defiance. Sigcawu was sent to prison. In protest,
a large crowd of his followers demanded to be impris-

oned with him, "because their chief could not spend a single day or night in a strange house without his attendants". The tribal bard says:

> Thou snake with ever-lengthening tail
> That impeded the house of the white men
> Even the houses of Meje and Madonele.

There are numerous other references of this nature in the praise-poems of this period. And an interesting feature about them is that the allusions to the exploits of any chief are not necessarily confined to his own praises. For instance, of the allusions to Mhlontlo that have been quoted, none appears in his own praises. They appear in the praises of contemporaries who were obviously taking a lively interest in what was going on elsewhere. This means that the vision of the tribal bards themselves was broadening, and their tribes had begun to regard themselves as units of a much bigger whole than hitherto.

The Church Bodies

The attitude of the African intellectual to the rivalry amongst the churches is best illustrated by an editorial in *Isigidimi* of August 1st, 1875.

> It amazes us to find people who should know how to live side by side in peace, who ought to forget that So-and-so belongs to this church, and So-and-so to that one, never cease to quarrel amongst themselves. As for us, this is one thing that we can never understand. We thought they had brought one Saviour, one God, because they carry one and the same book of scriptures, which will save any one who accepts it, no matter to

which church he belongs. These quarrels amongst the missionaries puzzle not only the Christians at the schools. Even the pagans are discussing them, wondering which one to believe. For a missionary belonging to a certain church comes to us and says: "Beware of the So-and-so's", where as these So-and-so's bring to us the same scriptures that he has been preaching. We remember a certain Sabbath Day when a pagan said, "Countrymen, we do hear you, but we are still at a loss. We don't know which God to follow, whether the Rhabe one (Presbyterian) or the Wesile one (Wesleyan).

Linguistics and Semantics

The intellectuals were now taking a lively interest in other languages too. The Xhosa people had only known Xhosa and English, and perhaps a little Dutch, while a very small section of theologians had been introduced to Greek and Latin. But the coming together of people in the industrial areas brought a number of African languages together. We therefore find an occasional article on the linguistic structure of some language or other, spoken in the diamond fields or some other centre. Rev. G. Tyamzashe, who was in Kimberley in the 1870's makes short comparative studies of Xhosa and Sotho, enumerates other languages spoken by the labourers there, and even attempts to group and classify them according to their grammatical structure.

This interest in languages results in a critical study of the Xhosa renderings of the scriptures. There are numerous articles discussing even the translations of words like: "Alas!" A discussion of the Xhosa equivalent of the word "conscience", results in a protracted controversy over several issues of *Isigidimi*, in which the participants discuss not only the derivations of the words suggested, but also the meanings of the equivalents in other languages.

But perhaps the most interesting of these controversies is that over the word "Thixo". Vimbe questions the use of this word for the Supreme Being. He argues that if there is only one God, as the scriptures claim, He should have one name only, and that name should be found in the language in which the scriptures were originally written; that is, Hebrew. The word "Thixo", he says correctly, is a Khoisan (Hottentot) word for a certain insect, and that the Xhosa people, copying the Khoikhoin, use it as a swear word when they sneeze! There are many participants in this controversy, some of whom are scandalized. The participants show an amazingly wide knowledge of languages. The words *Jehovah, Theos, Deus* and others are freely discussed. One writer reveals especial erudition. He shows how words even in a given language change their meaning. Among other examples, he cites the English word "cattle". According to him, the word in Elizabethan English meant *belongings.* Then later on the form "chattel" came into being, indicating lifeless possessions, as against live ones. After criticizing Vimbe, he concludes his article encouragingly, with a poem beginning:

I aim not to quench any gleaming light
In this land of shadow and darkness;
I deride not the light of a flickering star
When the sun and the moon are no more.

There being no light from the sun and the moon,
I will hail the lone star of evening,
And the flash of the floating fire-fly
Little bird that glows in the night.

10
Conflicts and Loyalties

IN a previous essay, we paid special attention to William W. Gqoba, the dominant literary figure of the earlier part of the 19th century. His poetry, as we have shown, reflects the social changes of his time. But in order to get as full a picture as possible of this epoch, some attention must be given to his lesser contemporaries, most of whom were far less ready than he was to accept the idea that the white people "gave up their homeland for love of us blacks". In fact, the Great Discussions—on Education and Christianity—would seem to have been an attempt on Gqoba's part to meet the sceptics of his time.

This period marks the most rapid, most drastic political, economic and social changes hitherto ever known by the Southern Africans. It marks the climax of the Wars of Dispossession; the final conquest of the Xhosa (1877), the Zulu War (1879) and the Gun War in Basutoland (1880–1881). Having been led to believe ᵗhat this was a conflict between Christianity and Paganism, or had made common cause with their "Christian brothers" against the "Pagans". But now they were doubtful about their own peculiar position in the new establishment.

In *Isigidimi SamaXhosa,* the monthly which was the main organ through which they could express themselves, many writers of this period give some attention to the war, its purpose and achievements. Somehow, this endless fighting, in which they often find themselves involved, is in conflict with the Christian idea of "peace and good will towards men". These doubts are aggravated by the actions of the conquerors, who seem always able to speak "with double tongue".

Writing about unemployment in Port Elizabeth, "L.L.D." relates that those who sought employment were told that there was road work to be done in Cradock. Transport was provided for those who wanted to go there, and a large number of men at once came forward. They were given two shillings each and told to climb on to the waggons. It was then learned some months afterwards that these men had never been taken to Cradock, but were packed off for compulsory military service.

In April, 1878, William Ayliff, Native Commissioner, made an announcement through *Isigidimi* that "women and children who took food to the Xhosa warriors in the fastnesses were to be shipped to Cape Town, to remain there until the war was over. Those of them who chose to remain in Cape Town could do so. When the war was over, the husbands and fathers would be shipped to Cape Town, free of charge, to claim their own".

What happened at the end of the war is to be found

in two articles. One is written by 'Hlati Lomtontsi' (Mtontsi Forest), who says:

What has anybody, whether black or white, Christian or Pagan, gained by this war? Yes, the white people perhaps may claim to have gained something, for don't we see little magistrates all over the land? But for us, blacks, the position is so bad that even those trustful people who always sang the praises of the large-hearted White Queen are silent. We were told that after the war, those men whose wives and children had been shipped to Cape Town would be allowed to go there at no expense to themselves in order to claim them. But what do we hear now? That instructions have been issued that no black male may be given a permit to travel to Cape Town.

An eyewitness of what happened in Cape Town wrote as "S.B.M." and said:

I write in tears. Children of the ages 3, 5, 6, and 10 have been hired out as servants. The mothers, who were kept at a place called the "Kaffir Depot", had no idea what had become of their children. This morning, I happened to be at the "Kaffir Depot" when five policemen came and ordered the women to pack up and board a ship which would take them to East London immediately. When the women refused to leave their children behind, they were forced out at point of bayonet. One woman actually took out a knife and tried to stab herself to death. But she was immediately seized and dragged like a log of wood to the docks where all the women were shipped amidst heart-rending cries.

In his aritcle, 'Hlati Lomtontsi' makes it clear that there is only one solution to this suffering. "Is it the spear? No, we have tried this and failed. The only solution is learning and knowledge. By knowledge I do not mean just book knowledge. I mean that kind of knowledge that will make us realize that each one lives for all.

Nor must this knowledge be confined to the males. Our young women must have it too. When you weed a mealie-field, you do not jump from one mealie-stalk to another, removing only those weeds immediately around the plant. You remove every weed whether it is near a plant or not".

I. W. W. Citashe, a poet of this period, writes in a similar strain:

> Your cattle are gone, my countrymen!
> Go rescue them! Go rescue them!
> Leave the breechloader alone
> And turn to the pen.
> Take paper and ink,
> For that is your shield.
> Your rights are going!
> So pick up your pen,
> Load it, load with ink.
> Sit in your chair,
> Repair not to Hoho,*
> But fire with your pen."

The few short stories written at this period make depressing reading. The rapid changes are undermining the African's manhood in all walks of life, and the writers are concerned with this rather than with entertainment. A story about "the King of Death" shows the havoc wrought by liquor. The King of Death issues a proclamation that he will award a prize to the courtier who brings the greatest number of subjects to his kingdom. A number of courtiers come forward and take turns in giving an account of their stewardship; among them, Asthma, Fever, Cyclone, Accident, and Liquor, in

*Mountain-forest stronghold where the Xhosa Chief, Sandile, was shot and killed.

that order. When Liquor enters, he is not steady on his legs, and his speech is thick. But he is sure of himself. He shows that he has served his king more loyally than the others have. Among other things he has made young men age before their time and die. He has picked on the most beautiful girls, destroyed their virginity, deprived them of their youth and beauty, and finally brought them to the King of Death. After listening to Liquor's account, the King of Death does not wait to hear any more. Satisfied that Liquor is the most loyal of all his courtiers, he awards him the prize.

Here then, we have the African writers now face to face with the military conquerer who lurked behind the missionaries. The earliest writers saw no connection between the two. But before the end of the century, the writers had begun to wonder if the interests of the spiritual and the military conquerors were identical. The sons of the missionaries now fill the "little magistracies", mentioned by 'Hlati Lomtontsi'. An occasional writer goes so far as to express some doubt as to whether the missionaries themselves are likely to remain long among the people. When a later writer, Mqhayi, said that Britain, "sent us the preacher and sent us the bottle; sent us the Bible and sent us gunpowder", he was expressing a disillusionment that had been felt as keenly, if expressed less artistically, by his predecessors fifty years before him.

11
The Harp of the Nation

IN the first few years of its life, from 1871 to 1878, *Isigidimi* was highly respected and trusted by the literate section of the Africans. Politicians, ministers of religion and lovers of general cultural progress paid tribute to it in prose and poetry. But with the sharpening of the struggle between black and white in the bloodiest period of the Wars of Dispossession, the people become disillusioned; and, by 1884, hardly any of the leading writers has a good word to say for the journal.

One of the most outstanding figures of this period was a contributor from St. John's Mission, Umtata, who styled himself "Hadi Waseluhlangeni" (The Harp of the Nation). The author of the poem whose first two stanzas (in translation) concluded a previous essay, "Hadi" was a highly respected writer of great intellectual integrity, widely read for that period in the literacy of the Southern Africans. It seems that no controversy could be brought to a close in *Isigidimi* until "Hadi" had made his contribution. If he did not write, either the other participants or interested readers suggested that it was about time that he did so. As a rule his contribution to any discussion was in the form of a prose essay, but he often concluded with a poem inspired by the subject under discussion.

When *Isigidimi* was adversely criticized by its readers, "Hadi" implored the editor to exercise patience. He commended *Isigidimi* for not losing heart in the face of such severe criticism, and likened the journal to a warrior at whom the enemy have hurled so many spears that his body becomes like that of a porcupine. Nevertheless, the warrior walks boldly on like an elephant:

> Press on to the heights of Ararat,
> Thy people borne bravely on thy back,
> Rescued from the torrent of ignorance.
> Be patient as a toiling mother
> Famished, but hoeing and weeding the corn,
> Her baby crying on her back,
> Her corn plants withering in the sun.

It must be remembered that the wars of this period include the War of Nchayechibi, against the Xhosa (1877–1878), the Zulu War (1879), and the Gun War, mainly against the Basuto (1880–1881). In *Isigidimi*, the whole struggle was made to appear to the Xhosa reader as a struggle between Heathendom, represented by *utshaba* (the enemy), and Christendom, represented by "our troops", "the troops of Victoria, Child of the Beautiful". Those Africans who were defending their land against the white invaders were cast as villains, and opposition to annexation and white domination was made to appear as hostility to "the progress of the

Word". Any reverse suffered by the white troops was greatly deplored, while every one of their conquests was hailed as "the triumph of the Word".

There is evidence in the letters to the editor that for a time the readers were infected by this propaganda— propaganda that successfully neutralized the African Christian intellectuals during the fighting. Indeed, one writer urged that as soon as any territory was conquered, the pagan chieftain should immediately be replaced by a Christian preacher. "Why should territory that has been won for Christ continue to be ruled by a heathen?" Even when the people in general wanted to revolt against the Act of Disarmament, one writer, Daniso Bulube, maintained that the blacks should be forbidden firearms until they had read the Bible! The first indications that the people had lost confidence in *Isigidimi* appear in 1881, when a Kimberley writer who styles himself *Ndingummbi* (I-am-a-digger) asks indignantly: "Whose messenger is *Isigidimi?*" He is followed by several others, including one Ndzeku who condemns *Isigidimi* as *ipepa elifileyo* (a dead paper).

It was not until April 2, 1883, after the editor had tried to defend himself against these attacks, that "Hadi" wrote as follows:

I am discussing the hostility that exists between *Isigidimi* and its readers across the Kei. The reason would seem to be this, that the younger intellectuals say they can never make out the true nationality of *Isigidimi. Isigidimi* never takes up a clear stand on political matters. It sides with the whites, for whenever a writer voices the feelings of the blacks, *Isigidimi* immediately makes him understand that he belongs to the side of the enemy. For instance, a writer who tried to put in a word for Langalibalele (a Hlubi chief) was quickly immersed under the waters of silence: while

another writer, who expressed the idea that Langalibalele was a mere goat trying to fight against an
elephant, was given praise and his words were echoed
far and wide.

In these days, when the nation is sickening to death,
in these days of long-lasting wars and short-lived
peace, it is demanded of you by the youth of your
fatherland that you give them the length and breadth
and depth of national news. Moreover, it is demanded
of you that you make a clearing in your paper, a clearing that you have to keep clean for men of conflicting
views, so that in this clearing they may discuss all the
matters that so affect their welfare and the welfare of
all the blacks. Only then shall we know what we are
doing. As a result of this practice, there will emerge in
this clearing national orators and bards, some praising
our side, and others praising the other side. Why cannot a bard emerge for once from the people of Mokha-
chane (Basuto) and sing as follows:

Arise, ye sons of the Mountain-at-Night!
The hyena howls, the white hyena,
All ravenous for the bones of Moshoeshoe,
Of Moshoeshoe who sleeps high up on the
    mountain.

Its belly hangs heavy and drags on the ground,
All gorged with the bones of warrior-kings;
Its mouth is red with the blood of Sandile.[1]

Awake, rock-rabbits of the Mountain-at-Night!
She darts out her tongue to the very skies,
That rabbit-snake with female breasts[2]
Who suckled and fostered the trusting Fingos,
Thereafter to eat them alive."

In the previous essay we mentioned the attitude of
the African intellectuals to the quarrels amongst repre-

1. Xhosa chief.
2. Queen Victoria.

sentatives of the various churches. The Africans would seem to have thought that it did not matter very much which church you joined, so long as you became a Christian. "Hadi" has a fairly long essay on this and kindred subjects.

The study of theology can never make one Christian body of us blacks. There are books and books on theology, and in their nature they are very polemical, and theology itself is a sea whose waves keep things assunder. Although they all sleep in one womb of the Bible, these books kick one another like Jacob and Esau in their mother's womb. Luther and Zwingli are the founders of Protestantism. They are one in their attitude to sin and in regarding the scriptures as the only true beacon of Faith. But in their theology they differed so much that Luther accused Zwingli of being a pagan . . . . If our forebears differed so much over theology, how can we hope to be united? The Protestantism that rescued us with a firm hand from the ignorant worship of the Roman Catholic Church has not the strength to bind us together into a unity like that of the Father and the Son.

The spirit of inquiry, which is our pride and the pride of these days, has torn the body of the church apart. Even the early leaders of the church, who met at large conferences and tried to put the body together, did not succeed. Instead of coming to some agreement, their views scattered in all directions like crackers on Guy Fawkes Day . . . . And yet the true children of God in the Presbyterian, in the Wesleyan and in the Anglican Church cry to one another wanting to worship together; but the heads of the church do not know where to find the needle and the thread that can sew together the shreds that they have created . . . .

"Hadi's" disillusionment with the churches appears in a poem he wrote for *Isigidimi* of February 1st, 1884, which begins:

Some thoughts till now ne'er spoken
Make shreds of my innermost being;
And the cares and fortunes of my kin
Still journey with me to the grave.

I turn my back on the many shams
That I see from day to day;
It seems we march to our very grave
Encircled by a smiling Gospel.

For what is this Gospel?
And what salvation?
The shade of a fabulous Hill[3]
That we try to embrace in vain.

In the same year, an article by *"Hadi Waseluhlangeni"* was rejected by the editor of *Isigidimi,* for being "too hostile to British rule". The great paper was dying indeed.

3. Another name for a *tikoloshe* (a spirit).

12

The Mounting Anguish

If *"Hadi Waseluhlangeni"* (The Harp of the Nation) was the outstanding writer of this period, he was not a Gulliver alone in Lilliput. There were several other writers of merit who were just as critical of the social derangement, just as outspoken as himself, if less erudite.

First there is "W. G.", who writes very bitterly about the mounting anguish of a subject people.

Why should a pass be forced upon people who have demonstrated in every way that they are loyal British subjects, people who remained *sleepers* (i.e., neutral) when their compatriots were fighting, people who remained with the Government and bore patiently all sorts of ugly, humiliating experiences? It is these people who are today deprived of their guns and forced to carry passes. And yet other British subjects still possess their guns, and now and again shoot people dead—by mistake, as they usually plead . . . .

Let there be some difference, now that we are British subjects. We cannot be made to carry passes when the white man does not. We cannot be deprived of our guns when the white man is not deprived of his. Our demands cannot be ignored when those of the white men are not. For we are equal under Queen Victoria, Child of the Beautiful. At present, however, this oneness is remembered only when money is required of us. Ah! when it comes to money, even the most aged woman is drained of her very last possessions . . . .

There is evidence in *Isigidimi* that the Xhosa-reading public has become familiar with Soga's translation of *The Pilgrim's Progress* by this time. Characters and incidents in this book are frequently referred to analogously. The Slough of Despondency, Vanity Fair, Apolyon, etc., have become bywords. An outstanding example is the analogous use of the incident of Giant Despair in a controversy about impending parliamentary elections. The writer, who remains anonymous, says:

Readers of *UHambo lo Mhambi (The Pilgrim's Progress)* will remember the story of Christian and Hopeful, the day they were found by Giant Despair. It is said that the giant put them into his castle, into a very dark dungeon, nasty and stinking to the spirits of these two men. Here, then, they lay from Wednesday morning till Saturday night without one bit of bread or drop of drink, or light, or any to ask them how they did. . . .

Now Giant Despair had a wife, and her name was Diffidence: who, when she heard about the prisoners, told her husband 'to beat them without mercy'. True enough, on the following morning they were beaten fearfully. The next night she, understanding that they were still alive, *"did advise him to counsel them to make away with themselves"*. Truly then, the giant did give them this advice, and again he beat them. But they, though tempted by his counsel, finally resolved not to accept it. *If they must die, it must not be by their own hands.*

We are reminded of this story by a number of men who are at present scattered amongst us, black folk,

counselling us how to get out of this slough, this dungeon of suffering into which our community has been
cast these past years. We have complained of laws that
oppress the black man alone: the branding of our cattle,
pass laws, disarmament without even adequate com-
pensation for our guns. We have complained of the
imprisonment of our ministers of religion, their being
arrested by the police while carrying out their duties to
the Word of the Lord. We have been pushed around by
so-called location regulations. These and other things
have been heavy on our necks, and many of them still
remain so, and we do not know what to do about them.
And now the time has come to elect men to go to
parliament. Among the men who are going to parliament there are those who are going there to add to the
burdens we already have. These men make no secret of
the fact that they still regard the black man as an
enemy, a thing to be treated as an enemy, a thing to be
deprived of education grants.

Today, it is those same men who have come to our
people and expect that it must be we ourselves who
send them to parliament. Hence, we say that they have
come to counsel us to do away with our own selves.
Giant Despair said, "I bring you counsel that will help
you when I say that you had better kill yourselves". In
like manner these men come smiling up to us and say,
"It is our ardent love for you that makes us say that you
had better elect us, the people who will truly destroy
you". Diffidence was enthusiastic about her counsel. In
like manner these men are enthusiastic about the counsel they bring to us.

It will be well for us to confer on this matter. The two
men we have used as an example conferred before they
resolved what to do. The day is very near when we
must resolve what to do, hence our suggestion that
there must be unanimity among those who have the
right to vote. For our part, we say we must not accept
the counsel to do away with our own selves. If we must
die, it must not be with our own hands.

The rejection of "Hadi's" article by *Isigidimi* (see
Africa South, Vol. 4, No. 2, Jan.–March, 1960) is not

taken lying down by other contributors. A letter by "G.K." writes as follows:

We complain particularly because, while refusing to publish Hadi's article, you Mr. Editor, undertook to reply to it. This is unfair to Hadi as well as to your readers. If you felt that you must reply, then surely you should have published Hadi's article, to enable intelligent readers to make their own judgement. This man Hadi never writes nonsense. I may tell you then that your comments (on the unpublished article) have only served to make our mouths water, and we so wish that we had read the article and drawn our own conclusions. Would that you had not made these petty comments of yours.

Evidence that the readers were keeping a watchful eye on *Isigidimi* is to be found also in a contribution made by Daniel Zondiwe on behalf of a group of malcontents in Tembuland. A representative of *Isigidimi* had visited certain parts of the Transkei and, on his return home, written a series of articles. In one of these, he lavished praises on a magistrate by the name of Levey, a very efficient labor-recruiting agent who had been popular in the Transkei till after the Gun War. In his reply, Zondiwe makes very graphic analogies, one drawn from the hunting methods of the Thwa ('Bushman'), and the other from the famous allegory of *Mother-Wasp and her Family* (found in a Xhosa Reader published at Lovedale). He writes as follows:

I want to say that the reason why you, Mr. Editor, think this magistrate is a good man is that you do not live close enough to him. If you were to live close to him just for one month, then you would know his spirit. Yes, he is good at handling court cases, but when it comes to political matters—never! He is the type of man who comes to the people as one of them, when, in fact, he is the enemy.

He is like a Thwa ('Bushman') hunting ostriches. They say that when a Thwa goes ostrich-hunting, he covers his body with an ostrich-skin to deceive the ostriches. Slowly he draws near them, now bending low and pecking the ground just as ostriches do, now ruffling his ostrich feathers. Then he goes this way and that drifting towards them, until he is so close that his arrow can reach them. Then he draws his poisoned arrow. Such a man is this *Livi* . . .

We have also heard the story of *Gxidolo* (Sloven), son of *Nomeva* (Mother-Wasp). He died of poisoning. It is related that when a certain man warned him that it was poison that he was drinking, he retorted, "Get away! What do you know? Do you think poison would taste so sweet? Never! Poison would taste bitter, like medicine!" But before he knew what was happening, his whole body was trembling, and his wings were paralyzed, and all he was able to do was to say in a hoarse voice, "Be kind enough to tell my mother how I met my death".

Such, then, is this man to those who think he is upright. "He is sweet, loving to our people, and would never betray them". It seems to me that we on this side (of the Kei) will awake one day to find our bodies trembling and our wings stricken with paralysis; and when we try to speak, all we shall be able to do is to say in hoarse voices, "This magistrate is not an upright man".

The mounting dissatisfaction with the policy of *Isigidimi* gives occasion to a fairly regular contributor who styles himself *Silwangangubo* (Eared Vulture) to recall with a certain amount of nostalgia the short-lived predecessors and contemporaries of this journal. He mentions *IKhwezi, Indaba, ISibutho Samavo,* and *UM-wesile,* which are all dead, and they died with a big mouthful of people's subscriptions.

But another contributor, Booi Kwaza, has no illusions about any of the Xhosa papers that have existed hitherto. He knows that they were all controlled by "foreigners". He is concerned about the young intellectuals who, after so much money has been spent on their education are not encouraged by senior compatriots to make their contribution to the cultural progress of their people. "What are we educating them for?" he asks. "If you lay an egg and abandon it unhatched, who do you think will hatch it for you?" He deplores the sorry spectacle of a whole people depending on milk from a "one-teated cow" *(Isigidimi),* and all of them jostling and elbowing one another in order to get at this one teat. "You can see", he says, "that amongst the white people the war is not being fought by means of sticks and spears, but by means of the pen and the brain. Countrymen, the time has come when something must be done by us—and it must be something other than the usual mutual bespattering. The time has come to find our young men something to do. The first thing we must acquire is a printing press".

Diplomatically, he says, "I do not look down upon *Isigidimi.* I admire it: I like it very much. All I am saying is that we must have a paper owned by the black ones, which it would not be a mistake to name 'ITembu' (Hope). I refer this matter to every black African".

Appendix

In essays 2 and 4, Professor Jordan refers briefly to the Xhosa writer, S. E. K. Mqhayi. When Mqhayi died in 1945, Jordan wrote a tribute which appeared in *The South African Outlook,* a tribute which contained a discussion and an assessment of Mqhayi's work.

This article is included as an appendix to *Towards an African Literature* because it is closely related to the contents of those essays.

Samuel Edward Krune Mqhayi *

Within three miles of the little township of Berlin, C.P., less than half-a-mile from the railway line between King William's Town and East London, is a hillock named Ntab' ozuko (Mount Glory). The hillock, as such, hardly deserves this dignified appellation. Indeed, twenty years ago it was known to the Ndlambe people as *IsiXhoba sikaTilana* (Tilana's Rocky Ledge)—Tilana being the name of the then occupant. This rocky ledge owes the name "Ntab' ozuko" to a more illustrious occupant, S. E. K. Mqhayi, late poet, novelist, historian, biographer, journalist, translator. It was on the summit of this hillock that he lived for nearly twenty years; it was there that he died on the 29th of July 1945; it is at its foot that his remains were buried on the 31st of July, exactly four months before he reached the age of seventy. During his life-time, Mqhayi produced the following books and pamphlets: *USamson* (a novelette), *ITyala lamaWele* (poetry and prose), *UDon Jadu* (a novel), *UmHlekazi uHintsa* (a poem in eight cantos), *ImiHobe nemiBongo* (poems for children), *InZuzo* (collected poems), *IBandla labaNtu* (poems), *IsiKhumbuzo sikaNtsikana* (essay on Ntsikana), *USogqumahashe* (biography of N. C. Mhala), *uBom bomFundisi uJ. K. Bokhwe* (biography), a free translation of *Aggrey of Africa* and his autobiography *UMqhayi waseNtab' ozuko.* One has reason to believe that one or two more works will be published posthumously. Mqhayi also published many historical essays through the press, and most of these are now included in the anthologies *Zemk' iinKomo maGwalandini* (ed. by Dr. Rubusana) and *ImiBengo* (ed. by Dr. Bennie) as well as in the Stewart Xhosa Readers.

In a short tribute of this nature, it is not possible to do justice to Mqhayi. A lover of the human race, he associated himself with several progressive movements and institutions. He understood alike the illiterate and educated, and as a result, his social influence was very wide. Because of his active interest in his people, his knowledge of their history, traditional and modern, was amazing. Through the press, by public orations, and in private letters, he had a message of encouragement to give to the social leaders of his people. One of the speakers at his graveside said, "If we should try to say all that can be said about the deceased, we should remain here till to-morrow morning, and still we should not have said all that can be said of him". The same can be said of his writings. His contribution to Southern Bantu Literature is easily the largest and most valuable that has hitherto been made by any single writer.

Mqhayi was born on the banks of the Tyhume on the 1st of December, 1875. He attended school at Evergreen, in the Tyhume Valley, at the age of seven. During the three years at this school he met three of the men who were destined to influence his whole life and career. These were the Rev. E. Makhiwane, the Rev. P. J. Mzimba and Mr. J. Tengo Jabavu. In 1885 he accompanied his father to his new home in Centane (Kentani) and remained there for six years. Then he came to attend school at Lovedale where he received some training as a teacher before he went into the world. His literary career began in East London, when, with the encouragement of Dr. Rubusana, and Messrs N. C. Mhala, A. K. Soga, and G. Tyhamzashe—all of them distinguished leaders of the time—he began to contribute *izibongo* (praise poems) and historical information to the periodical *IZwi labaNtu* (The Voice of the Bantu). Later on he became sub-editor of this paper, but circumstances compelled him to return to teaching, and for many years he served as a teacher among the

Ndlambe people. Then he became editor of the *Iim Vo zabaNtsundu,* but even this he had to give up after some time and go back to teaching. This time he was offered a post at his *Alma Mater,* Lovedale, but during the few years in the world Mqhayi's views on South African history and how it should be taught in African Schools had undergone such modification that he found himself compelled either to be false to his own convictions and teach history as the authorities would have him teach it, or to give up teaching altogether. He decided on the latter. On leaving Lovedale he went to make his home on the "summit" of Ntab' ozuko—a Mount Helicon whence he descended in his impressive kaross on great tribal or state occasions to sing the praises of important personalities. The last of such occasions was the meeting held by the Minister of Native Affairs at King William's Town last July.

We owe a great deal to the six years in Centane. For it was during this time that Mqhayi began to understand the culture and history of his people. It was there that he saw *imidudo, iintlombe, intonjane, imiyeyezelo, amadini,* etc. As he relates, he used to sit spell-bound, listening to *inkundla* orations. It was there that he first listened to *izibongo* and himself began to "lisp in numbers," praising favourite oxen, other boys or himself. It was there that he began to appreciate the beauty, dignity and subtleties of Xhosa, and to acquire the amazingly wide vocabulary that even Tiyo Soga would have envied. But this does not mean that he spent all his time among the "heathens." He and his sister often accompanied the Rev. J. M. Auld on his visits to the schools for purposes of inspection of Religious Instruction, and Mqhayi won a number of Sunday School prizes at this time. He also attended the local day school, but had to remain in Std. III during all those six years because no inspector ever came to promote the pupils! This many-sided education explains a very interesting feature of Mqhayi's life and writings. Because he was nurtured in Christian culture and in the primitive culture of his own people at the same time, Christianity was for him not an "escape from the City of Destruction," but a mode of life abundant that was not irreconcilable with his native culture. Small wonder then that Tiyo Soga's translation of *The Pilgrim's Progress* should have had such an appeal for him that at the age of thirteen he was able to recite its first chapter with such feeling and expression that many who listened to him at an elocution competition at the Station School at Lovedale feared that "much learning hath made him truly mad."

To discuss all his writings is impossible. We shall therefore refer to his masterpiece, *ITyala lamaWele,* to his prose work *UDon Jadu,,* and lastly to his poetry in general. *ITyala lamaWele* includes fiction, history and poetry. The book owes its title to the novelette that covers its first half—the lawsuit of the twins. The plot of this novelette is suggested by Verses 28–29 of the 38th Chapter of the Book of Genesis. As the author states in the preface, the purpose of the story is to give a picture of legal procedure among the Xhosa people, and to show the democratic spirit in which it is carried out. A civil dispute has arisen between Babini and Wele, twin-sons of Vuyisile, born under circumstances similar to those described in Genesis, Chapter 38. Having lived at a headman's kraal for six years as a boy in Centane, Mqhayi is conversant with legal procedure. The stating of the case by the plaintiff, his cross-questioning by the councillors, the calling-in of witnesses, the *hlonipha* language used by the mid-wives in submitting evidence, the declamation of the bard at the end of each session, the reaction of the men to *izibongo,* the unassuming manner of the sage Khulile as he makes an exposition of the principles underlying the law of primogeniture, the pronouncement of the verdict and Chief Hintsa's sympathy with the senior twin in pronouncing it, the humble but dignified manner in which Babini receives the verdict given against him—all these give a beautiful picture of social life among the Xhosa during the reign of Hintsa. It is these and the beauty and dignity of the language that give this novelette its fascinating power and such a high place in Xhosa Literature. Mqhayi is not a great creator of individual character. Hardly any character stands out in this story, and consequently the impression left in the reader's mind is the collective dignity and refinement of the chief and his subjects.

In the latter half of the book, fiction and fictitious characters disappear, and we have true history. The "death" of Khulile synchronizes with the arrival of the Fingos from the east and of the news of a white race coming "from the sea". The relations between the Xhosa and these new-comers, the diplomacy exercised by the White men in driving a wedge between the Xhosa and the Fingos on the one hand and between the two rival sections of the Xhosa on the other, the mutual jealousies and the bitter rivalry that broke the unity of the Xhosa and contributed towards their downfall—all these are related with commendable restraint by Mqhayi. In beautiful style he traces the fortunes of the Xhosa people beyond the "emancipation" of the Fingos, beyond the death of Hintsa, beyond Sarili's exile, beyond Maqoma and Sir Harry Smith, right up to the acceptance of the new loyalties and to the disaster of the *Mendi,* by which time the subject is no longer the Xhosa alone, but the Bantu of South Africa in general. The book closes with short biographies of the new leaders of the "reaction to conquest". An interesting feature is the bard's own development. The poetry in this book punctuates the prose, each piece being appropriate to the incident under consideration. In the lawsuit as well as in the early chapters of the history, the versification, in keeping with the theme, is in the style of the traditional *izibongo,* but with the acceptance of the new loyalties by his people towards the close of the book, the bard himself begins to experiment in modern versification. Therefore, to be fully appreciated, *ITyala lamaWele,* though partly fact and partly fiction, partly verse and partly prose, must be viewed as a whole. Then it has the effect of a great epic drama in which the bard, like a Greek Chorus, comments upon, or predicts, the fortunes of his people.

Next to *ITyala lamaWele,* Mqhayi's most important prose work is *UDon Jadu.* Through the influence and guidance of Don Jadu, a highly educated African, the *amaRanuga* (detribalized Africans) of the Eastern Province acquire land of about the area of the Transkeian Territories. All kinds of industry begin to spring up in this new province of Mnandi (Sweetness). As a result, in a few years the population is double that of the Transkei. The Union Government becomes interested, and vote large sums of money to promote the scheme. Self-government is granted to the people of Mnandi and, the Union Government having disappeared from the scene, Great Britain assumes guardianship. Don Jadu is the first president.

There is neither racialism nor isolationism in Mnandi. Immigration is encouraged, and experts of all races and shades of colour come from the four corners of the earth to make a permanent home there. There is full social, economic and political equality. According to the constitution, women are free to go into parliament, but the sensible women of Mnandi decline this offer on the grounds that there is enough work for them to do at their homes! Mnandi is a Christian state, and Christ is the "President" of the Ancestral Spirits. Ministers of religion are officers of state, and their stipends come from the general revenue. Magistrates and ministers of religion work in close co-operation. In fact, Church and State are so closely knit together that there is no distinction between the police and deacons' courts. Education is compulsory. Xhosa is the first language, but English is such an important second language that no one who is not strictly bilingual may hold an office of state. Baby boys are baptized and circumcised in the Temple eight days after birth, and Holy Confirmation forms part of an initiation ceremony held in the Temple between the ages of fifteen and twenty. All these ceremonies are supervised by the magistrate and the minister of religion together. The marriage ceremony is conducted by the magistrate and subsequently blessed by the minister of religion. Divorce is prohibited by law. The importation or sale of liquor is prohibited by law. Home-brewing is allowed, but anyone found drunk in public places is locked up in a lunatic asylum, dressed in the uniform of the asylum and is for seven days subjected to the same treatment as the legitimate inmates of that institution. People who are sentenced to penal servitude receive wages for their labour. There are no prisons.

UDon Jadu makes very interesting and thought-provoking reading. It is true that in constructing a "bridge" between our present South Africa and his Utopia, the author idealizes away a few hard facts, but—

> its soul is right,
> He means right,—that, a child may understand.

If we turn to his poetry, we find that Mqhayi, though perhaps possessing more talent, is nevertheless more limited in scope, than some of the younger Nguni poets. Essentially a poet of the traditional type, for theme he is almost wholly confined to concrete subjects, usually human beings. He is confined to lyrical verse, chiefly odes and elegies. Even historical themes he was never able to put into narrative verse. If he had been able to write narrative poetry, we can almost be sure that the poem entitled *UmHlekazi uHintsa,* instead of consisting of eight cantos disappointingly lacking in unity, should have been an epic. Again, it is a pity that in his later writings he decided to break entirely with the diction and artistic formlessness of *izibongo* in favour of modern versification. With his limited knowledge of prosody it was only natural that he should not be able to go much further than discover rhyme—of all the artificial ornaments of Western versification the most obvious, and yet to Bantu the least desirable. A sense of effort and strain is always with us when we read his rhymed verse, and very often we feel that in order to observe rhyme, the poet has sacrificed sense, virility and easy flow of language. His favourite rhyme scheme is the heroic couplet, and because he invariably writes end-stopped lines, his rhymed verse makes dull and monotonous reading.

But if we judge Mqhayi by what he has achieved instead of judging him by what he has failed to achieve, then there is no doubt that his best poetry is of a high order. To understand him, let us remind ourselves that one of the essential qualities of *ubumbongi* was true patriotism, not blind loyalty to the person of the chief, but loyalty to the principles that the chieftainship does or ought to stand for. On public occasions *imbongi* had not only to praise the chief but also to criticise him by means of those epithets and metaphors that make such an interesting characteristic of *izibongo.* Obviously then only a man who took genuine interest in the social welfare of his people can be *imbongi.* Mqhayi possessed this quality, hence his being known as *ImBongi yesiZwe Jikelele,* which title was conferred upon him by a Zulu in Johannesburg. But Mqhayi had a double loyalty. As a Xhosa he was loyal to the Xhosa chiefs and their ancestors, and as a British subject he had to be loyal to the British king. A poem written during the Boer War in the *IZwi labaNtu* of March 13th, 1900, shows how very sincerely Mqhayi had accepted British guardianship. Each stanza has a refrain, *"SingamaBritani!"* (We are Britons!). Nurtured in Christianity and in the policy of the "Old Cape Liberals", he believed that the conquest of Southern Africa by the British was the working out of a Divine Purpose. After the defeat in 1879, he makes the Zulus say in the poem *ISandlwana:*

Wozani, maBritani, sigezan' izingozi;

(Come, ye Britons, let's bathe one another's wounds!)

Then the Zulus go on to tell the British that their own defeat was the working out of God's purpose, so that from the British, the Zulus might receive a new life, a new birth, a new learning, and see the Love of the Son of the Great-Great, and fight His battles.

But the Act of Union drove the "Old Cape Liberals" to the background, and representations to Britain did not receive the usual kind of reception. Britain was forgetting that she had "children" in Africa. So the poem written in praise of the Native Labour Contingency of 1916, *umKhosi wemiDaka,* opens with the significant lines:

> *Awu! Ewe, kambe, siyabulela,*
> *Lakuth' ikokwethu lisicinge,*
>
> . . . .
> *Ngexesha lalo lokuxakeka.*

(O yes! We must feel honoured, I suppose, that our father has remembered us in his time of need.)

But Mqhayi has not quite lost faith in the British connection. In the elegy written on the disaster of the *Mendi,* though bemoaning the loss of the flower of Africa, he reminds his people that some such worthy sacrifice had to be made if they truly loved Britain; he reminds them how God sacrificed His own Son, the Messiah. Again the working-out of a Divine Purpose! If the ties with Britain are not to break, as they threaten to do, this sacrifice must be.

Ngoko ke So-Tase! kwaqal' ukulunga!
Le nqanaw' uMendi namhlanje yendisile,
Naal' igazi lethu lisikhonzile.

The last word in the second line, *yendisile,* is very
eloquent. *Ukwendisa* is to give one's daughter in marriage, and those who know the mutual obligations between the families involved in a marriage-contract as
Mqhayi understands marriage, will understand how
strong should have been the ties, according to him,
between Britain and the Africans after the disaster of
the *Mendi.* But the Victorian Days were gone, never to
return, and, if anything, Post-Union South Africa was
threatening to undo all the good that Mqhayi had seen
in the Victorian Policy. It is therefore in true *imbongi*
spirit, and as a patriot praising and criticising a chief in
public, that in praising the Prince of Wales in 1925,
Mqhayi, after a succession of metaphors and similes, in
which he likens the prince to all the mighty fabulous
animals of Bantu Folklore, should utter words which
may be translated as follows:

> Ah, Britain! Great Britain!
> Great Britain of the endless sunshine!
> . . . .
> You gave us Truth: denied us Truth;
> You gave us *ubuntu:* denied us *ubuntu;*
> You gave us light: we live in darkness;
> Benighted at noon-day, we grope in the dark.

Mqhayi has written several religious poems, on
Christmas, on the Gospel, and on kindred subjects.
Perhaps the best illustration of his deep-seated religion
is to be found in the closing lines of a poem entitled
InTaba kaNdoda, written in praise of a little mountain

peak near King William's Town. A poem of forty lines, it closes as follows:

> Would that I had tongues, O Mount of my home
> O footstool of the God of my fathers,
> Thou, whose brow, facing the setting-sun,
> Is smitten by the rays of the closing day.
> So would I, protected, sing thy praise;
> So would I, forsaken, fly to thee,
> And kneel in humble prayer by thee,
> Who art the stepping-stone between me and my
>   God.
> Still shall the aliens stare not understanding,
> While, praying, on this slope I build a ladder,
> And scale the vast fatiguing heights, to kiss
> The Feet of God the Father—Creator, Most High.

"Nature for Nature's sake" hardly has a place in *izibongo* of the old type, and Mqhayi's nature poems are on the whole disappointing. But this does not mean that he was blind to the beauties of nature. Scattered here and there are couplets that reveal not only his sensitiveness to the beauties of nature, but also his genius for the "precious word":

> Imizi yalo mlambo niyayibona na
> *Ukutyityimba* yakombelelwa yingxangxasi!
> (Lo, how the rushes on the waterside
> Thrill to the music of the cataract!)
> Kunqanqaza oonogqaza emathafeni,
> *Kukhenkceza* iinyenzane equndeni.
> (Grass-warblers clinking in the fields,
> Cicadas shrilling in the meads)
> Ndee *ntshoo-o!* ntshobololo-o-o!
> Ndaxel' inkwenkwez' ingen' elifini.
> (Sliding away, sliding away I go,
> Like a meteor swimming into a cloud.)

If this article has shown that Mqhayi was the soul of his people, and that to understand him is to understand their hopes and aspirations, then it will have served its purpose. Mqhayi takes the highest place in Xhosa literature. He has done more than any other writer to enrich Xhosa. In his hands it receives a fresh impress, and he has revealed all its possibilities as a powerful medium of expression of human emotion. His prose as well as his poetry contains expressions that became proverbial long before his death. If much of his verse will soon be forgotten, and for many generations to come, his prose style will remain something for younger writers to emulate. And now, as the Meteor slides along and swims into the Dark Cloud that must for ever hide it, let us hope that the younger generation has caught its splendour, to cherish and to carry to the great New Age that Mqhayi must not know.